W9-AEK-915

GLOBE
HISTORICAL CASE STUDIES

SOMOS MEXICANOS

MEXICAN AMERICANS IN THE UNITED STATES

Globe Fearon Educational Publisher
A Division of Simon & Schuster
Upper Saddle River, New Jersey

CONSULTANTS

José Carrasco is Chairperson of the Mexican American Studies Department at San Jose State University. He received his Ph.D. in the sociology of education from Stanford University. He has both taught and worked in the social sciences with an emphasis on Mexican American studies, education, social work, and humanities. He is nationally recognized in the fields of community organization and leadership development and currently serves as a consultant to the Pacific Institute for Community Organization (PICO).

Stephen De Leon Casanova is a faculty member for the Division of Bicultural/Bilingual Studies at the University of Texas at San Antonio, where he teaches courses in Mexican American studies. He is currently completing his dissertation in educational policy studies from the University of Wisconsin. He has worked as a journalist specializing in issues concerning the Chicano community. He was a member of the Chicano movement and has remained active in the Mexican American community.

Dolores González-Engelskirchen is currently the Director of the Illinois Administrator's Academy, where she provides state mandated training for city principals and administrators. She has taught and managed an elementary school bilingual education program. She also served as Principal of Chopin Elementary School and as Sub-District Superintendent in the Chicago Public School system. She received her undergraduate degree from Northern Illinois University, and her M.S.Ed from Chicago State University.

Fernando Rivera is the Social Studies Department Chair at Madera High School in California, where he also teaches Chicano studies. He holds a B.A. in Chicano studies/political science and an M.E.D. in bilingual education. He is also an active member of the Mexican American Teacher's Association.

Executive Editor: Jean Liccione
Market Manager: Rhonda Anderson
Senior Editor: Karen Bernhaut
Production Editor: Alan Dalgleish
Editorial Assistants: Ryan Jones and Derrell Bradford
Electronic Page Production: Sharon Ferguson, Mimi Raihl, and Heather Roake
Photo Research: Jenifer Hixson
Series and Cover Design: Joan Jacobus
Designer: Lisa Nuland

Printed in the United States of America 1 2 3 4 5 6 7 8 9 10 01 00 99 98 97

ISBN: 0-835-92267-7

 Globe Fearon Educational Publisher
A Division of Simon & Schuster
Upper Saddle River, New Jersey

CONTENTS

There are more than 17 million Mexican Americans in the United States today. They express pride in their nation as well as in their Mexican heritage.

BRIDGING TWO CULTURES

TERMS TO KNOW
- indigenous
- Indios
- haciendas
- Criollos
- Mestizos
- vaqueros
- Latinos
- Anglo

They were a poor people. Living in a desert land in what is today northern Mexico, they barely scraped a living from the land. They called themselves the Mexica. We know them today as the Aztecs.

Many years ago, deep in the mists of history, the Mexica decided to move to the South, where the land was better for farming. Their legends tell what happened next.

As they prepared to move, one of the Mexica priests told the people of a recent dream. In the dream, the war god had given his people a command. The Mexica were to search until they found an eagle sitting on a cactus, eating a serpent. On that spot they were to build their new home.

For more than a hundred years, the Mexica pushed south. Each time they found a good place to live, they were chased away by more powerful people. Then they entered a large valley surrounded by mountains. One day, walking along the shores of a lake, a Mexica priest noticed an amazing sight on a small island.

There, atop a cactus was a large eagle. In his beak was a black snake! On this island in the middle of a lake, the Mexica began to build their new home. It was from these modest beginnings, legend says, that the mighty empire of the Aztecs grew.

1 Mexico's Brilliant Heritage

The story you have just read is part history and part myth. Some of it can be proved. Some of it was made up over time to explain events the Mexica did not understand. Like many other peoples, the Mexica merged both myths and facts in their histories. The story of the Mexica has had an enormous influence on both Mexicans and Mexican Americans.

The ancient name, Mexica, became the name of the valley in which the people lived. The people also gave their name to the country of Mexico to which they contributed so much.

The eagle eating a snake has become a central symbol of modern-day Mexico. It is on the flag of Mexico and adorns many buildings. It has also become a respected symbol of modern-day Mexican Americans. In the 1960s, Mexican American farm workers organizing a strike created a banner with the Aztec eagle at its center. You will read about the farm workers' struggle in Case Study 5.

Other Advanced Cultures

Even before the rise of the Aztecs, there were other advanced cultures in Mexico. In the south, the Maya built great stone cities and temples. Mayan cities were dominated by stone pyramids. Some of them were as tall as 20-story buildings. The Maya were skilled craftspeople. They had a very advanced understanding of the movement of the stars and planets, which helped them create an accurate calendar. They used the calendar to schedule planting, harvests, and religious ceremonies.

From the Maya, the Toltecs learned how to build. They used this knowledge to construct beautifully carved stone cities. When the Aztecs entered the valley of Mexico around the year A.D. 1325, they adopted many of the religious beliefs and skills of the Toltecs.

"An Enchanted Vision"

At first, the Aztecs lived in very humble circumstances on islands in the lake. But the Aztecs were skilled warriors. Over time, the Aztec army conquered other groups in the valley of Mexico. At its height, the Aztec empire stretched over a vast area of central Mexico.

The Aztecs demanded large payments from all the conquered peoples. Corn and fish, cloth and feathers, gold, silver, and precious jewels all flowed into Tenochtitlán (teh-nawch-teet-LAHN), the Aztec capital city.

Tenochtitlán was one of the world's most beautiful cities. It had handsome public buildings surrounded by gardens and trees. It had great pyramids and a network of canals that cut through the city. Tenochtitlán was also an engineering marvel. Workers toiled for years, building roadways to connect the many islands that made up the city.

In 1519, Tenochtitlán was as big and as busy as any European city. One Spaniard who saw it in that year reported:

> Gazing on such wonderful sights, we did not know what to say or whether what appeared before us was real. . . These great buildings, all made of stone, seemed like an enchanted vision. Indeed, some of our soldiers asked whether it was not all a dream.

The historic meeting between Spanish conqueror Hernan Cortés and the Aztec emperor Montezuma is shown in this picture. This meeting forever changed the history of Mexico and the Americas.

Stripping the Conquered Land

The Aztecs believed their empire would last forever. Then, one day in 1519, messengers raced to the city with startling news. A group of light-skinned strangers had landed on the east coast.

The Aztecs thought that the leader of these strangers must be their great god Quetzalcoatl (ket-sahl-koh-AH-tuhl). They believed that one day Quetzalcoatl, who had left the Aztecs, would return from the east. Believing the strangers to be representatives of the god, the Aztecs let them enter the empire.

The strangers were actually Spanish conquerors, and their leader was Hernan Cortés. When fighting broke out between the Aztecs and Spaniards, the Aztecs were defeated. They could not defend themselves against the Spaniards for several reasons. First, the Spaniards used the horses and guns they had brought from Spain in battle. The Spaniards also brought another powerful weapon from Spain—smallpox. This disease killed many Aztecs. Moreover, the many peoples that the Aztecs had conquered and enslaved fought with the Spaniards to defeat the Aztecs. In 1521, after 80 days of fighting through the streets of the city, the Aztecs surrendered to the Spaniards.

After defeating the Aztecs, the Spaniards stripped the empire of gold and other treasures. The Spaniards took the land of many **indigenous**, or native, peoples. In Mexico, indigenous peoples are often referred to as **Indios**. In the United States, they are usually referred to as Native Americans.

The Spaniards called their new empire New Spain. They divided the land into **haciendas**, or large estates. In 1545, they discovered huge veins of silver in New Spain. Vast new wealth flowed to Spain. The few who ran the colony of New Spain became extremely wealthy.

Indios, on the other hand, suffered at the hands of the Spaniards. The Spaniards made Indios work on the haciendas or in the mines as slaves. Indios were overworked and exposed to new diseases. They died in vast numbers.

Roman Catholic missionaries set out to bring their religion to the Indios. The missionaries wanted to convert Indios to the Catholic religion. However, their methods were often harsh. The Spaniards also imposed their language and culture on the Indios. They attempted to destroy the culture of the Indios.

The Wealth of New Spain

In the 1600s, Mexico City, the capital of New Spain, glittered with wealth. Carriages trimmed in gold and silver clattered down stone streets. Elegantly dressed men and women strolled past fountains and flower gardens. Printing presses published a wide range of books.

The wealth and culture of New Spain contrasted sharply with other European settlements in North America. Far to the north, settlements such as Jamestown (founded in 1607) and Plymouth (founded in 1620) were little more than collections of mud huts.

A System Set in Stone

The Spaniards established a social system in New Spain that favored the few people who were born into high positions. Their wealth was built by the work of the vast majority of people who were born into poverty.

At the top of the social scale were people who had been born in Spain. They held all the highest offices in the government and the Church.

One step below them were the **Criollos** (kree-OH-yohs), who were people born in the Americas to Spanish parents. The Criollos could not hold high positions in the Church or government. However, many of them were very wealthy.

The next class of people were **Mestizos,** people whose parents were of mixed Spanish and Indio background. Many of them worked on the haciendas. Others were craftspeople in the cities.

At the bottom of society were Indios and Africans. As you have read, many of these people worked as slaves under brutal conditions.

Moving Toward Independence

Spain tried to keep tight control over its colonies. It crushed any attempt of the people in New Spain to win freedoms. In 1541, a group of Indios called the Zacatecas rose in revolt. The revolt was brutally put down. After the revolt, the Zacatecas who survived were sent to work as slaves in the mines.

Although New Spain barely changed over the years, the outside world was changing quickly. Two new values, democracy and freedom, were emerging. The Spanish empire would not long survive when these values reached its colonies. The American Revolution (1775–1783) in the British colonies made people in the Spanish colonies want their own independence from Spain. The French Revolution (1789–1795) spread ideas of equality to the Spanish colonies.

In 1810, the spark of revolt exploded in New Spain. There, a gentle Catholic priest in the little town of Dolores decided to take action against the Spaniards. His name was Father Miguel Hidalgo y Castilla.

The Cry of Revolt

After years of serving his parish, Father Hidalgo joined a plot against the Spaniards. Warned that the Spaniards were coming to arrest him, Father Hidalgo refused to flee his village.

On the morning of September 16, 1810, he hurried to the church in Dolores and rang the church bell. When the townspeople were assembled, Father Hidalgo began speaking. He shouted:

Down with bad government. Down with the Spaniards!

Father Hidalgo talked of the injustice that Mexicans faced and demanded that Spain grant Mexico its freedom. His cry of freedom sent shock waves through New Spain. Large numbers of Mestizos and Indios joined his force. This rebel army of 50,000 swept through town after town, seizing Spanish officials and throwing them in jail.

The Spanish government sent an army to crush the rebels. Just outside Mexico City, the rebel army put up a fierce fight. But it was no match for the well-trained Spanish troops. Father Hidalgo and other leaders were captured and executed by a firing squad.

Final Victory

New leaders emerged after the death of Father Hidalgo. As the revolt spread, many Criollos joined it. They were afraid that the revolt would be successful—and they would be left out. It took 11 bloody years before the Spaniards were driven out of Mexico. In 1821, the people of Mexico finally won their independence. At the same time, other revolutions had broken out all over Latin America.

Independence changed the government, but it did not end the old social divisions. Mexico was still a land of a few rich people and many poor people. The Church and the army held tremendous power. Millions of Indios were without land and without rights. Not until the rise of an Indio named Benito Juárez did Mexico begin to give power to the powerless. You will read about the heroic Juárez in Case Study 2.

Thinking It Over

1. How did the Spaniards manage to defeat the Aztecs?
2. **Evaluating Information** Why do you think Mexicans today see the arrival of the Spaniards as a turning point in their history?

2 In El Norte

After conquering the Aztecs, the Spaniards searched for new lands to conquer. They heard tales of mountains of silver and golden cities to the north. Soon Spanish settlers headed out toward el Norte, the North, to find their fortunes. They settled in many areas of what is today the southwestern United States.

New Mexico: A Blending of Cultures

In 1610, Indios living along the east bank of the Rio Grande heard the rumbling of wagons and the sound of Spanish voices. Peering into the dust, the Indios saw hundreds of men, women, and children riding and marching toward them. At the front of the strange group rode soldiers in glittering armor.

The group of Spaniards stopped at a place close to the mountains. There, a cold stream provided an important source of water for crops and animals. In the summer of 1610, work began on this settlement, which became known as Santa Fe. Santa Fe struggled to survive for many years. In 1680, an Indio revolt drove out the Spanish settlers. The Spaniards fought for 12 years to restore control.

Slowly over the years, the settlement began to grow. By 1776, Santa Fe was a thriving and beautiful town. The settlers built adobe homes, which kept them cool in summer and warm in winter. Whitewashed churches glowed in the sun. The Indio and Spanish cultures blended in Sante Fe and throughout New Mexico. Soon, Mestizos outnumbered both the Spanish and the Indio populations.

By 1776, communities were established in what are now the modern cities of El Paso, Texas; Albuquerque and Taos, New Mexico; and Tucson, Arizona.

Texas: Settling the Great Plains

In 1718, a group of priests and soldiers arrived at a river in central Texas. On its west bank they built the mission of San Antonio de Valero. The mission later became better known as the Alamo.

At first, the little mission barely survived. Indios were slow to move there because of disease. However, in 1731, the Spanish king sent about 200 farm families to San Antonio de Valero. This outpost later became the modern city of San Antonio.

Toward the end of the 1700s, the Spaniards began to realize the true wealth of the Texas plains. They discovered that the region was perfect for grazing wild cattle and horses. New settlers began moving to Texas. To encourage settlement, the government gave large grants of land to wealthy Spaniards who would settle there.

These estates were worked by **vaqueros** (vah-KEE-yeh-rohs), rugged Mestizo or Indio cattle herders. The vaqueros developed the way of life that comes to mind today when we think of American cowboys.

California: A Land of Plenty

California had been settled by Roman Catholic missionaries at the beginning of the 1700s, but it wasn't until the 1760s that the government of New Spain pushed settlement hard. News of Russian and British ships near the northern coast of California worried the Spaniards. They wanted to make sure that these two nations did not claim California.

In 1769, the Spaniards founded a settlement in what is today San Diego. During the next 50 years, the Spaniards built a number of forts and missions along the coast of California. In the missions, missionaries taught Indios how to grow grapes and other crops common in Europe. The missions attracted Spanish settlers to the region. Many of these settlers brought cattle and started ranches. In Case Study 1, you will read about the cultured life that developed among the Californios, the Mexican settlers of California.

Between Two Worlds

By the beginning of the 1800s, the Spanish government had built settlements throughout California, Arizona, New Mexico, and Texas. Most of the settlers were Mestizos and Indios.

With the end of the Mexican American War in 1848, the United States took over one half of Mexico's territory. With a stroke of the pen, Mexicans in these settlements suddenly became foreigners in their own land. Once again, they had to struggle with new laws and new customs.

The Alamo was no more than a humble mission when it was founded in 1718. As the region became more populated, the city of San Antonio was founded.

Thinking It Over

1. What industry became important on the plains of Texas in the 1700s?
2. **Summarizing** How did the Spanish settlements in New Mexico, Texas, and California change life for Indios who lived there?

3 Mexican Americans in the United States

It is hard to imagine what the United States would be like today without the 17 million Americans whose heritage is Mexican. Mexican Americans form one of the largest ethnic groups in the United States. They are also one of the oldest. Nearly one and a half million Americans today can trace their heritage back to Mexicans living in the U.S. Southwest before 1848.

The Mexican American heritage is alive and thriving today. We can see it in the hundreds of fine old buildings that were once missions in the American Southwest. Many towns, cities, states, rivers, and mountains in the United States have Spanish names. These places are home not only to people of Mexican ancestry, but also to people whose ancestors came from all parts of the globe.

The largest populations of Mexican Americans are in California, Texas, New Mexico, Arizona, and Colorado. There are also large Mexican American communities in Illinois, New York, Oklahoma, Oregon, and Washington State. To give you some idea of the importance of Mexican Americans, consider this: the number of Mexican Americans living in the city of Los Angeles is larger than the number of Mexicans living in any city except for Mexico City.

What's in a Name?

What does the term *Mexican American* mean? A Mexican American is any citizen of the United States whose ancestors were born in Mexico.

As you have read, many Mexican Americans have ancestors who lived in the southwestern states long before this area was part of the United States. However, more than 10 million Mexican Americans have ancestors who moved to the United States from Mexico. Many Mexicans came to the United States during the Mexican Revolution, which began in 1911.

You will read about the Mexican Revolution and one of its greatest heroes, Emiliano Zapata, in Case Study 3.

The Roots of La Raza

People often mix up the terms *Mexicans* and *Mexican Americans*. They don't realize that there is a difference between the two. Mexicans are citizens of the nation of Mexico. Mexican Americans are citizens of the United States who have a Mexican heritage.

Americans with Mexican ancestors do not all agree on what to call themselves. Some people in New Mexico refer to themselves as *Nuevo Americanos* or *Hispanos*. In Texas, the term *Tejanos* is often used. Many young Mexican Americans in California and Arizona use the term *Chicano* as a badge of pride. No matter what they call themselves, most Mexican Americans consider themselves to be part of *La Raza*, a Spanish word meaning "the race." This term expresses a feeling of community spirit which unites people of Mexican heritage.

Mexican Americans are part of a larger group of people known as **Latinos**. Latinos are American citizens whose roots lie in Spanish-speaking lands south of the United States. These lands include Mexico, the nations of Central and South America, and many islands in the Caribbean Sea.

The term *Anglo* originally meant Americans whose ancestors were from England. Today, the term is sometimes used to describe Americans whose background is from anywhere in Europe except Spain. In this book, we use the term *Anglo* in this way.

The Role of Language

At the root of the Mexican American culture is the Spanish language. Although most Mexican Americans speak Spanish, English is the first language for many Mexican Americans.

Whatever language they speak, Mexican Americans live in a nation in which the Spanish language has had an important impact. We have mentioned numerous places in the United States with Spanish names. To this list, we can add all the Spanish words that have entered the English language in the United States. Many of them come from the vaquero, or cowboy, experience. Such words as *ranch, rodeo, chaps,* and *stirrups* all come from Spanish words that the vaqueros used.

The Mexican American Presence

As loyal citizens of the United States, Mexican Americans have fought bravely for their country. You will read about some of these people in Case Study 4. Many more have fought for justice within their own community. In Case Study 5, you will read about Dolores Huerta, who worked to improve conditions for farm workers. Case Study 6 examines the social and political accomplishments of the Chicano Movement. Case Study 7 describes how Mexican American women living in East Los Angeles took bold action to protect their neighborhood.

The United States and Mexico

Relations between the United States and Mexico have sometimes been tense. Today, relations between the two countries are much warmer, and the two countries are bound by strong ties of culture and trade. In Case Study 8, you will read about how Mexico and the United States have tried to increase trade and business along their shared border, and the issues this has raised.

Thinking It Over

1. What is the difference between a Mexican and a Mexican American?
2. **Formulating Questions** What questions about Mexican history and Mexican American culture do you hope to have answered in this book?

In January 1848, gold was discovered in northern California. The discovery drew thousands of people to the region, forever changing the state's history.

CALIFORNIOS AND THE GOLD RUSH

CRITICAL QUESTIONS

- How did the United States gain control of California from Mexico?
- How did the California Gold Rush change life for Mexican Americans?

TERMS TO KNOW

- Californios
- ranchos
- migration
- manifest destiny
- placer mining
- squatters

ACTIVE LEARNING

Imagine that you are a Californio at the time of the Gold Rush. Take notes about the events that are happening and how they have affected your life. At the end of the case study, you will use these notes to write a letter to friends in Mexico, telling them how the Gold Rush has changed your life. As you read this case study, look for the Active Learning boxes. They will offer you tips for note taking.

Sitting tall in the saddle, wide-brimmed hat perched low on his head, the cowboy has become a well-known symbol of American history. Books, television programs, and films often celebrate cowboys as heroes of American culture. People around the world recognize the cowboy as an important part of the American experience.

Would it surprise you to learn that the cowboy is not an American invention? The original American cowboy is actually the vaquero (vah-KEE-eh-roh) — the Mexican cowboy who worked the ranches of California and the southern plains centuries before the term *cowboy* even existed.

As far back as Spanish colonial times, vaqueros helped raise and round up cattle on lonely ranches. Without the vaqueros, it would have been impossible to run these huge estates. They also learned to live and fight on the backs of horses. Their courage and skills became famous.

"To be a vaquero," went one saying, "is to be a hero."

To this day, many of the words we associate with American cowboy life come from the vaquero experience. Such words as *ranch, rodeo, lasso, corral, chaps,* and *stirrups* all come from Spanish words that the vaqueros used.

It seemed that the vaquero way of life on California ranches would never change. However, it was destined to completely change in the middle of the 1800s. The change began one day in 1848 when a carpenter saw a speck of gold shining at the bottom of a shallow stream in northern California.

1 Home on California's Ranches

Ignacio Villegas was a young vaquero on his father's ranch in central California. The family arrived from Mexico City in the early 1840s, when Ignacio was eight years old. Young Villegas started doing adult jobs at an early age, riding the boundaries of his father's land and helping to round up the cattle. Like most boys and girls in California, Villegas learned to ride horses when he was very young. In a book about his life, Villegas recalled,

> There were no roads to speak of, only trails, and for many years, horseback was the principal means of travel.

The Villegas family led a lifestyle that had existed in California for several centuries. Mexican families who had lived in California before it became part of the United States were known as **Californios**. Many were descended from original Spanish settlers, and they lived on **ranchos**. Ranchos were ranches, or huge estates on which the Californios raised large herds of cattle.

The Californios: A Rich Tradition

The ranch on which Ignacio Villegas lived was east of Monterey Bay in a town called San Felipe in central California. The Mexican government had given his father the land for the ranch. The government was very generous to a few well-connected individuals.

A Good Movie to See

Vaquero: The Forgotten Cowboy, PBS Video, 1988 (60 minutes)

Vaquero: The Forgotten Cowboy is a documentary that celebrates the unsung hero of the American West, the Mexican American vaquero. The film traces the origins of cowboy life to the first Spanish settlers. It also gives an exciting portrait of the proud, present-day vaqueros.

Owning the ranch had brought the family great wealth. Villegas's father employed large numbers of vaqueros, both Mexican and Native American, to manage the cattle on his ranch.

Wealthy families, such as the Villegas family, usually had many children. At a young age, both boys and girls were trained to ride horses and use a lasso, a long rope used to catch horses and cattle.

The children of wealthy Californios often had private tutors who educated them and taught them other skills. Many children became expert dancers, musicians, and writers. Villegas was fortunate enough to have received an excellent education. He would later use what he had learned to write his book of personal experiences.

As the years passed, the Californios came to see themselves as different from Mexicans. California was removed from the outside world. It seemed to many Californios that their prosperous way of life would go on forever.

Active Learning: Make notes for your letter about life in California before the Mexican American War. Include details about the life of the vaqueros and the education of Californios.

In the Borderlands

In 1845, Mexico was a young country. It had been independent from Spain for only 24 years. California, or Alta California as it was called, was a distant province of Mexico.

As far back as 1521, Spanish settlers had brought the first cattle to the Americas. More than 300 years later, most Californios were raising cattle and sending the hides to factories in Boston. There, the hides were made into shoes. The trade in cattle hides brought much wealth to the Californios.

Wealthy Californios enjoyed a way of life that was cultured and privileged. However, most Mexicans in the region were poor. While Californios were sending their children to Mexico City or Europe for an education, most people in Alta California could neither read nor write. They lived in poverty on ranches or in poor villages.

When the poor compared their lives with those of the wealthy, they often felt great resentment. During the 1830s and 1840s, the poor staged a number of uprisings against the ranches and other settlements in California.

Though the wealthy Californios called on the government in Mexico City to send help, it did not come. The central government

Vaqueros, or Mexican cowboys, were expert horsemen who managed large herds of cattle. El rodeo, or the summer cattle roundup, was the highlight of the year for a vaquero. At el rodeo, vaqueros roped horses and cattle, and rode untamed mares. These contests became the model for the modern rodeo.

considered California to be too far away to waste troops on. The Californios themselves put down the uprisings, often with great force.

To Mexican government officials, California was the "borderlands"— a faraway frontier area of little importance. Thus, the Californios could not rely on the government when they most needed its help. On the other hand, the remoteness gave the Californios a good deal of independence from Mexican rule. The Californios became used to governing themselves without Mexican interference.

The Mexican American War

After years of paying little attention to California, the Mexican government suddenly became concerned about this faraway territory in the mid 1840s. The increased **migration**, or movement, of Americans to California alarmed the government.

"California is entirely at the mercy of the North Americans," stated a Mexico City newspaper in 1845.

The concerns of the Mexicans were well founded. The United States had already annexed, or taken over, Texas in 1845. Texas had won its independence in 1836. After independence, it applied to join the United States as a new state. After some debate, Congress admitted Texas as the nation's 28th state.

Many Mexicans predicted that U.S. ambitions would not stop with Texas. They worried that the United States would try to seize California and New Mexico, as well.

The prediction came true. Under the leadership of U.S. President James Polk, the United States declared war on Mexico on May 13, 1846. The aim of the war was to expand U.S. borders so that the country would stretch from the Atlantic ocean to the Pacific ocean.

The United States called this policy **manifest destiny**. The policy was based on the American belief that the United States had a manifest, or clear and obvious, destiny to grow westward.

What the Americans saw as destiny, the Mexicans saw as land theft. The Mexicans believed that the war was part of an American plan to steal land from a smaller country.

The Mexican American War lasted for almost two years. Finally, on February 2, 1848, the two countries signed a treaty in the town of Guadalupe-Hidalgo, outside Mexico City. The treaty ended the war.

The Treaty of Guadalupe-Hidalgo

With a stroke of the pen, Mexico lost about half its territory in the treaty. The United States acquired the territories that now form the states of Arizona, California, Nevada, Utah, and half of Colorado and New Mexico.

The treaty offered U.S. citizenship to those Mexicans who wanted it. It gave people a year to decide if they wanted to retain their Mexican citizenship or become U.S. citizens. Whether or not they became U.S. citizens would not affect their rights. They could remain in the United States no matter what they decided to do. The treaty also promised that the United States would fully protect the property rights of Mexicans who stayed in California after the war, whether or not they chose to become U.S. citizens.

However, as you will read, the treaty was not enforced. Anglo, or white Americans, treated the Californios as foreigners. Even those who had chosen to become citizens of the United States were treated as outsiders.

Blending Legal Systems

When the United States took over California, it kept some of the Mexican laws that had governed California before the war. One such law gave women the right to buy and sell land. Based on that law, all property owned by a woman before marriage remained her individual property. This right was preserved in California

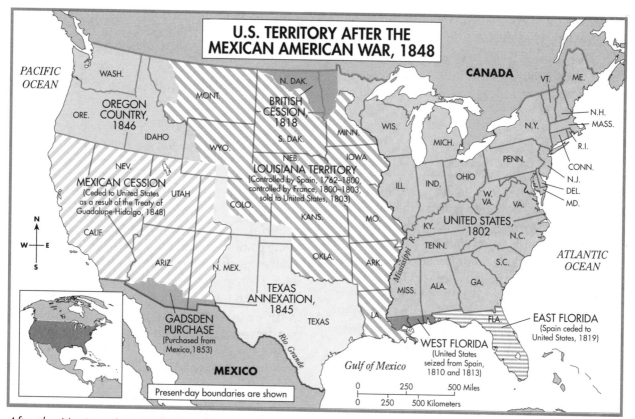

U.S. TERRITORY AFTER THE MEXICAN AMERICAN WAR, 1848

PACIFIC OCEAN

WASH.

OREGON COUNTRY, 1846

ORE.

IDAHO

MONT.

N. DAK.

BRITISH CESSION, 1818

CANADA

VT. ME.

N.H.

MASS.

WIS.

S. DAK.

MINN.

MICH.

N.Y.

PENN.

R.I.

CONN.

N.J.

DEL.

MD.

WYO.

NEV.

NEB.

IOWA

LOUISIANA TERRITORY
(Controlled by Spain, 1762–1800, controlled by France, 1800–1803, sold to United States, 1803)

ILL.

IND.

OHIO

W. VA.

VA.

MEXICAN CESSION
(Ceded to United States as a result of the Treaty of Guadalupe-Hidalgo, 1848)

UTAH

COLO.

KANS.

MO.

KY.

UNITED STATES, 1802

N.C.

CALIF.

TENN.

ATLANTIC OCEAN

N
W—E
S

ARIZ.

N. MEX.

OKLA.

ARK.

S.C.

GA.

MISS.

ALA.

GADSDEN PURCHASE
(Purchased from Mexico, 1853)

TEXAS ANNEXATION, 1845

TEXAS

LA.

WEST FLORIDA
(United States seized from Spain, 1810 and 1813)

FLA.

EAST FLORIDA
(Spain ceded to United States, 1819)

MEXICO

Rio Grande

Gulf of Mexico

Present-day boundaries are shown

0   250   500 Miles

0   250   500 Kilometers

After the Mexican American War, the United States gained a large amount of land. What territories did the U.S. gain after the war? What other lands had the U.S. won or purchased from Spain or Mexico before the war?

after it became part of the United States. It would have a big impact on future settlers from the East, where women did not enjoy this right.

Thinking It Over

1. What rights were Mexican citizens promised in the Treaty of Guadalupe-Hidalgo?
2. **Predicting Consequences** What effect do you think the Mexican American War would have on future relations between Mexico and the United States?

2 Gold Fever!

James Wilson Marshall could not hide his excitement. "Gold! Gold! Gold—at least three-carat gold!" he told people in the first rush of excitement. His discovery at Sutter's Mill in northern California took place in 1848, only nine days before the United States and Mexico signed the Treaty of Guadalupe-Hidalgo. Mexico signed away to the United States a region rich in gold and other minerals!

The discovery of gold was pure accident. John Sutter had hired Marshall, a carpenter, to build a sawmill near a stream in northern California. One day, while Marshall was inspecting the work, he saw something glittering in the water. He said:

> There was about a foot of water running then. I reached my hand down and picked it up. It made my heart thump, for I was certain it was gold.

Gold! Gold! Gold!

Marshall and Sutter tried to keep the news from spreading. They hoped to gain all the riches for themselves. However, once the news was out, it proved impossible to contain it. As soon as one of the cook's children heard the story, he told his parents, who told another worker. The news of the gold discovery spread like wildfire.

When news of the discovery reached San Francisco, newspapers ran enormous headlines. Bakers left bread baking in the oven and teachers walked out of classrooms to rush to the gold fields.

Quickly, the news spread eastward to the rest of the United States and southward into Mexico. Soon, thousands of Americans and Mexicans had arrived in California. Each one had his or her own special dream of striking it rich. Gold fever seized the world. Soldiers and sailors deserted their posts by the hundreds to rush to California. People in South America, China, Australia, and Europe joined the rush. The population of California exploded from 15,000 in 1848 to 260,000 only four years later.

Travel by Land and Sea

To get to California from the East Coast, travelers had to make a long and hard trip. Some people traveled by foot. Others traveled on ships that went down to Panama or around the southern tip of South America.

The Hesters were one of the many families that had chosen the overland route. Their wagons were loaded with a cooking stove made of sheet iron, a portable table, tin plates and cups, and cheap knives and forks. They also had their own food, medicine, guns, and tents, all packed into a wagon nine feet long by four or five feet wide.

On April 27, 1849, Sally Hester wrote this entry in her dairy: "As far as aye [eye] can reach, so great is the immigration, you see nothing but wagons."

Cooperation—At First

As they arrived in California to make their fortunes, many newcomers from the East discovered to their horror that they knew almost nothing about mining. On the other hand, many of the Californios and new arrivals from Mexico were experienced miners. Mexicans had been mining silver and gold for several hundred years.

At first, Californios and the recent arrivals from Mexico helped Anglos and others learn to pan for gold. **Placer mining**, finding gold by washing soil and gravel, was difficult work, and it required experience. The Mexican miners taught the Anglo miners how to use a batea, a flat-bottom pan, which filtered out the water and dirt and left the large pebbles.

In the beginning, gold was plentiful, and it was relatively easy to pick gold nuggets from river beds. In these first days, there was a sense of cooperation between miners.

That cooperation soon vanished. After the big nuggets were taken, it became harder to find gold. Naturally, the more experienced Californios and Mexicans were more successful at panning gold from streams. This success made the Anglo miners angry. Bloody fights often broke out between Anglo and Mexican miners. With the tide of migration bringing new miners from the East to California every day, the Anglos soon outnumbered the Mexican and Californio miners.

Staying Out of the Gold Fields

As these newcomers poured into California, other ways to make a fortune opened up. In fact, most of the people who grew wealthy from the Gold Rush were those who did not pan for gold.

The new arrivals were mostly men who had come to California without their families. They needed food, clothing, tools, and a place to sleep. Since they were busy searching for gold, they counted on other people to provide them with these services. Many of the people who provided these services were Californios. During the early days of the Gold Rush, the ranches prospered. California's exploding population needed to be fed. Beef became the food of choice for many of the newcomers. At its peak, the price of cattle rose to $100 a head, just about what it cost to buy a house.

As you have read, Ignacio Villegas's family had its ranch in San Felipe, near the Monterey Bay. This was also near a popular route for gold prospectors arriving from Sonora, Mexico. The family took advantage of this location by opening a store and a restaurant. The restaurant could serve 20 people at a time. Because travelers were hungry and food was scarce, the Villegas family could charge high prices. A meal at the Villegas's restaurant cost as much as 50 cents, a hefty sum at the time.

Other merchants met the needs of the new arrivals by offering other services at high prices. A newspaper cost only a nickel in the eastern states. At one time, California newspapers sold for $1.50. Other merchants charged up to $2.50 for delivering a letter. After being away for months, gold seekers eager to hear from their families were willing to pay high prices.

Foreigners Do Not Have the Right to Mine

As digging for gold became more difficult, the competition grew fierce. The Anglo miners became suspicious of "foreigners." They argued that these "foreigners" should not be allowed to "steal" a precious national resource like gold. To them, foreigners included Californios. They ignored the fact that the Treaty of Guadalupe-Hidalgo had given citizenship to Californios and others. In their greed, these Anglos vowed to drive out all the "foreigners."

A Californio named Antonio Franco Coronel saw this prejudice first hand. In March 1849, Coronel wrote in his diary about a frightening experience. He reported:

> I arrived at the Placer Seco and began to work at a regular digging. Shortly, we received news that it had been resolved to evict [force out] all those who were not American citizens from the placers. It was believed that the foreigners did not have the right to mine the placers.

Soon, about 100 Anglo miners invaded his digging area. Some were armed with pistols, knives, and rifles. They forced him and other Californios and Mexicans to run for their lives.

By 1849, the scene described by Coronel was becoming more common. Less than a year after gold was discovered, the Anglo population of California had reached 100,000. This total compared to only 13,000 Mexicans. By force of numbers, the Anglos dominated the land and the state legislature. They were in no mood to respect the rights that Californios had been granted by the Treaty of Guadalupe-Hidalgo.

Active Learning: Make notes about the discovery at Sutter's Mill. Include details that describe the behavior of people after the discovery and what changes it brought to California.

A Tax on Foreigners

Californios and Mexicans soon became targets of much discrimination. Anti-foreign posters began to appear in mining towns. In 1850, the California Assembly asked the U.S. Congress to bar all foreigners, including Californios, from the mines.

In May 1850, the California state legislature passed a foreign miners' tax law. This law placed a special tax of $16 a month on all foreigners. Included among the foreigners were the

At first, Anglos and Californios mined for gold side-by-side. Californios and Mexican miners often taught Anglos how to mine for gold. As gold became harder to find, however, Anglos began to treat Californios and other non-Anglos harshly. Eventually, many Californios were driven from their land.

Californios. Even though the law was not strictly enforced, it threatened to bankrupt any miners but the Anglos.

Later in 1850, there were outbreaks of mob violence against Californios and foreigners. As a result, many Californios and foreigners left the gold fields. The foreigners could at least return home. To the Californios, California *was* home. They had nowhere else to go.

Violence against Mexicans became widespread. One Mexican woman was captured by an angry mob in the town of Downieville. It was never clear if she had actually committed a crime. There was only a rumor that she had stabbed an Anglo who had broken into her home. Based on that report, she was immediately arrested, tried, and hanged in front of a mob of 1,000 people.

As the violence increased, Mexicans fought back. Joaquín Murieta came to California during the Gold Rush. His exploits in the next few years are part truth and part legend. It is impossible today to separate the truth from the legend. Murieta supposedly turned to crime after miners killed his wife.

In Calaveras County, Joaquín Murieta's name caused such fear among Anglos that any Mexican who looked like him was considered dangerous. For Latino people, however, Murieta was considered a hero because he rebelled against the injustices committed by Anglo miners.

3 The Struggle Over Land

Most people who came to California in search of gold did not find it. Many went broke trying to make their fortunes. Most left the gold fields but stayed in the state.

Having given up on the idea of finding gold, some Anglos decided to become ranchers or farmers. However, they did not own any land in California. The land the Anglos wanted belonged to the Californios.

As you have read, the vast majority of the Mexican American population in California did not own any land. Rather, land ownership rested in the hands of a few wealthy families. One such family was the Vallejo family.

Taking the Land

Before the Mexican American War, Mariano Guadalupe Vallejo was one of the wealthiest Californios. He owned more than 200,000 acres of land in Sonoma Valley. A wealthy and cultured Californio, he had welcomed the Anglos during the war and offered them hospitality. But after the Gold Rush, the new Californians forgot his hospitality. His land became a target for Anglos who wanted it for themselves.

Many Anglos resented the fact that wealthy Californios owned large ranches. The Anglos wanted that land for their own use. Some became squatters, illegal occupants, on the ranches owned by Californios. In an effort to drive Vallejo and other Californios off their own land, Anglos burned their crops, shot their cattle, and tore down their buildings.

The Anglos demanded that the huge ranches be divided into smaller plots that could be distributed to Anglos. They did not understand that large tracts of land were necessary to support a herd of cattle in California's dry climate.

Anglo squatters did not treat Vallejo and other Californios with much respect. They ignored the parts of the Treaty of Guadalupe-Hidalgo that granted legal and property rights to Californios. Instead, Anglos acted as if all the lands of California were theirs by right of conquest.

There was much confusion regarding ownership of land. In the past, when the United States had taken over other territories, the government had granted land to new settlers. Many Anglos who settled in California were expecting a similar offer.

Proving They Owned the Land

Some of the problems Californios faced were due to differences between the Mexican and American laws of land ownership. U.S. laws required that land titles and land surveys be precisely laid out and perfectly accurate.

To the Americans, the records established under Mexican rule seemed sketchy. In Mexico's legal system, land ownership was based largely on how long the farmer had occupied and used the land. Boundaries were often not precisely drawn out. Land could be sold by verbal agreement. There was often no need to record sales officially.

Because of these differences, Californios generally had trouble proving that they owned the land. Many Anglo squatters filed lawsuits, hoping to use the American legal system to take land away from the Californios. Californios found that under U.S. law, their land could be taken away even though they had lived on that land for many generations.

In the 1890s, Vallejo wrote of these troubled times. He said:

One of the leading American squatters came to my father and said, "There is a large piece of land where the cattle run loose, and your vaqueros have gone to the gold fields. I will fence the field for you at my own expense if you will give me half."

The elder Vallejo agreed, but when the fence was built, the squatter registered the land in his own name.

Said Vallejo sadly:

In many similar cases, American settlers in their dealings with the ranchos took advantage of the laws which they understood, but which were new to the [Californios] and robbed the latter of their lands. [Written contracts] were considered unnecessary by a Spanish gentleman, as his word was always sufficient security.

Squatters found support from state senator William M. Gwin. In 1851, he proposed a new California law that created the Board of Land Commission. This law required that all landowners appear before the board to prove their titles. This violated the Treaty of Guadalupe-Hidalgo, which had guaranteed Californios ownership of their land. Suddenly, Californios had to prove that they owned their land.

This development gave confidence to squatters. They could remain in occupied lands, hoping that the rightful Californio owners would not be able to prove their titles. In effect, Californio landowners were considered to be liars until they could prove that they really owned the land.

Legal Battles Won and Lost

It took some Californios more than 17 years to establish their titles through the legal system. Even when they won, they lost—either because the process cost them their entire savings or because squatters destroyed their land.

Vallejo fought for his property rights. However, his legal battles were time-consuming

Mariano Vallejo is pictured here with two of his 16 children (back row) and three granddaughters. Vallejo was one of the wealthiest Californios.

and costly. Vallejo finally won his land claim after appealing to the U.S. Supreme Court. However, squatters refused to move from his land and destroyed his crops.

Vallejo's brother managed to prove his land claim before the Land Commission after paying his lawyers $80,000. Penniless, he finally sold his property and moved to San Francisco.

In the end, neither the Treaty of Guadalupe-Hidalgo nor the legal battles were enough to protect the property rights of the Californios. In the long run, control of the best farming lands of California passed largely into the hands of Anglos.

A New Culture Emerges

By the end of the Gold Rush, Californios had seen their rights and property taken away. Many Californio families were forced to leave

California after losing their land. Many felt that they had become foreigners in their own land. Others stayed, such as Mariano Guadalupe Vallejo. He later served as a state senator after California became a state.

The Gold Rush had drastically changed the population of California. The new Californians were mostly young and male. Only one out of every 12 newcomers was a woman. The number of women would not come close to the number of men until the year 1900.

As you read earlier, one of the most immediate needs of the new population was for newspapers. Hundreds of newspapers began to publish in California. Some of them were bilingual, or written in two languages: English and Spanish. One such paper was *The Californian,* published first in Monterey, then in San Francisco.

A new culture began to emerge in California. It mixed Anglo and Mexican ways. This new culture inspired many Californians to write poetry and short stories that appeared in these bilingual newspapers.

Perhaps the best known of the bilingual newspapers was a Los Angeles newspaper called *El Clamor Público,* The Public Outcry. It was started by a 20-year-old journalist named Francisco P. Ramirez. Besides carrying news, it suggested ways that Mexican Americans could fight for their rights. The paper also urged schooling for girls as well as boys. To help its readers learn English, *El Clamor Público* carried messages of pride and hope to the Spanish-speaking community.

In the years to come, Mexican culture and Anglo culture would continue to mix and influence each other in California. For example, in the state and elsewhere in the Southwest, Anglo cowboys adapted the boots and hats of the Mexican vaqueros who had preceded them. The vocabulary used by vaqueros also became part of the language of the United States. Even the vaqueros' musical tradition was adopted by English-speaking cowboys.

Active Learning: Take notes about the struggle for land resulting from the Gold Rush. Include information about land ownership changes and the Treaty of Guadalupe-Hidalgo.

A Continuing Influence

The political power of Mexican Americans began to grow after the Gold Rush, particularly in Los Angeles, where Mexican Americans outnumbered Anglos. Californios often filled important government positions. For example, Juan Sepúlveda was named to the city government of Los Angeles, and Antonio Franco Coronel became the first school superintendent in that city.

The power of Mexican Americans in California politics has grown considerably in recent years. Today, Mexican Americans are an important voice in California politics. They continue to carry on their traditions, which blend the ways of Mexico and the Californios with the ways of Anglo society.

Thinking It Over

1. What methods did Anglos use to take land from the Californios?
2. **Drawing Conclusions** How did the U.S. legal system hurt the claims of Californios to their land?

GOING TO THE SOURCE

Working Together to Pan for Gold

Photographs can help you understand a period of time in ways that words sometimes cannot. Pictures provide clues to the past and a feel for the time. They show us how people and places in recent history looked. The picture below shows people of different ethnic groups working together at a gold panning site in California. Study the picture and then answer the questions that follow.

From Ketchum, Liza. *The Gold Rush*. Boston: Little, Brown and Company, 1996, p. 96.
Credit: Henry E. Huntington Library, Dag #55

1. What does the picture show? What kind of clothes are the people wearing? What tools are they carrying?
2. **Drawing Conclusions** Do you think this picture was taken early in the Gold Rush or later? Explain your answer.
3. **Interpreting a Photograph** What kind of lives do you think gold miners lived?

Case Study Review

1. What rights were the Californios guaranteed under the Treaty of Guadalupe-Hidalgo?
2. What were the differences between Mexican land laws and American land laws?
3. How did the differences between Mexican land laws and American land laws affect the Californios?

Working Together

Form a small group with three or four classmates. Review this case study and choose one event or scene that your group would like to write about. Create a short newspaper article about it. Write a newspaper headline to go with the article. Include key facts related to the event. You may want to add an illustration or drawing to your article. Use your school or local library for additional resources.

Active Learning

Writing a Letter Review the notes you took as you read this case study. Create an outline of the letter you are going to write about how the Gold Rush changed your life as a Californio. Your letter does not have to include all the details covered in this case study. However, you should include a description of what life was like before the Gold Rush and what major changes took place afterwards. After you prepare your outline, write the letter as if you were addressing friends in Mexico.

Lessons for Today

Although many were American citizens, the Californios were often treated as foreigners by Anglo settlers. Why do you think it is difficult to unify a country in which people of different cultural backgrounds live? Do you think people in other countries have the same attitude? Write a brief essay explaining your point of view on this matter.

What Might You Have Done?

It is 1850. You are a Californio whose land is occupied by squatters. You do not want to lose your land and are willing to put up a legal battle. But, at the same time, you also know that the legal battle can be costly and you may not win. What would you do and why?

CRITICAL THINKING

Analyzing a Primary Source

Historians often use **primary sources** to learn about the past. A primary source gives first-hand information about people and events. Primary sources include letters, diaries, political documents, and newspaper editorials. Personal memoirs, paintings, photographs, and editorial cartoons are also primary sources. The primary source below is a section from the Treaty of Guadalupe-Hidalgo of 1848. Read it and answer the questions below.

> *Article VIII. Mexicans now [living] in territories previously belonging to Mexico, and which remain for the future within the limits of the United States. . . shall be free to [stay where they are] or to [move back to Mexico], retaining the property which they possess . . . or disposing [of it] . . .*
>
> *Those who shall prefer to remain in said territories, may either [remain] . . . Mexican citizens, or [become] citizens of the United States. But, they shall be under the obligation to make their election within one year. . . and those who shall remain. . . without having [made a decision] . . . shall be considered to have elected to become citizens of the United States.*
>
> *In the said territories, property of every kind, now belonging to Mexicans not established there, shall be inviolably respected. The present owners, the heirs of these, and all Mexicans who may hereafter acquire said property by contract, shall enjoy with respect to it guarantees equally ample as if the same belonged to citizens of the United States.*

1. What choices did Californios have for citizenship according to the Treaty of Guadalupe-Hidalgo? How long did they have to make their decisions?

2. According to the treaty, what happened to property belonging to Californios?

3. According to what you have read in the case study, did Anglos respect the terms of the treaty? Explain.

Many Mexicans regard Benito Juárez as Mexico's greatest leader. He devoted his career to helping the poor.

BENITO JUÁREZ: BUILDER OF MODERN MEXICO

CRITICAL QUESTIONS

- How did Benito Juárez save his country when it was torn by civil war?
- What reforms did Juárez make to strengthen democracy in Mexico?

TERMS TO KNOW

- reforms
- Liberals
- Conservatives
- inauguration
- epidemic
- vaccinations

ACTIVE LEARNING

As you read this case study, you will create a timeline of the history of Mexico that spans the life of Benito Juárez. At the end of the case study, you will add events that took place in the United States. As you read, take notes about events and dates mentioned in the case study. Also, look for the Active Learning boxes. They will offer tips to help you complete your timeline.

Just before dawn on a December morning in 1818, the boy arose from his straw mat into the cold darkness. He moved quietly so he would not wake his uncle, who was sleeping on a mat on the other side of the room. Silently, the boy put on his clothes and slipped out the door.

The boy shivered as he felt the cold, but he put his head down into the winds and walked quickly down the dirt path leading out of town.

Twelve-year-old Benito Juárez had been thinking about this adventure for some time. However, leaving was not an easy decision to make, and he had been torn by conflict. On the one hand, there were his friends and his uncle. He knew he would miss his friends. He loved his uncle, Bernadino, and did not want to hurt him. After all, Bernadino had raised Benito since he was six years old. On the other hand, the boy desperately wanted an education. He knew there was no way to get that education in his village.

Later, Juárez would write:

I decided before very long that only by going to the city could I learn anything more. I often asked my uncle to take me there, but he always replied "We'll go there someday," but he never made a move to begin the journey.

Two days before he left, Juárez had made up his mind to go by himself to the city, Oaxaca (wah-HAH-kah). His sister had gone there two years earlier to work as a servant at the home of a family named Maza. She would help him.

By the time the sun had begun to rise, Juárez was well into the mountains. Wearing a ragged straw hat and worn clothing, he had little protection against the mountain winds.

On he walked through the forest slopes, and soon the morning became afternoon. Now he started to feel hungry, but he had no food.

The sun was just going down behind the treetops when he reached a rise and saw below him the city of Oaxaca. There were homes in all directions and of all colors — not mud huts like the ones in his village, but large, brightly colored homes. There were plazas and churches and other large buildings whose purpose he could not begin to imagine. Somewhere down there in one of these homes was his sister. But in which one did she live?

It was well into evening when a very tired and hungry Benito Juárez entered Oaxaca. He had no money. He spoke only a few words of Spanish and could not speak any Mixtec, the language used by most of the Indios who lived in the city. Wherever he went in the city, he asked for Josefa, his sister, and Maza, the family for whom she worked. Finally, a stranger recognized the family name and led him to the grandest house he had ever seen. Josefa opened the door. Her mouth dropped open in surprise when she saw her brother. Benito Juárez was ready to begin his new life.

1 Juárez *Is Mexico*

Mexicans consider Benito Juárez Mexico's greatest leader because he fought all his life for justice for the poor. He rose from the most desperate poverty to become president of Mexico. As president, he held his country together during a time of civil war and fought an invasion by French troops. He believed strongly in democracy, and he worked throughout his life to strengthen it in Mexico. Juárez was the first leader to improve conditions for Mexico's Indios and Mestizos. As a recent president of Mexico has said: "To Mexicans, Benito Juárez *is* Mexico."

The story of Benito Juárez had its roots in extreme poverty. Juárez was born in a small mountain village in southern Mexico in 1806. Both his parents died when he was three years old. Juárez was raised first by his grandparents and later, by his uncle, Bernadino.

Like most people in the village, Juárez spoke only the language of his Indio heritage, Zapotec. As a child, Juárez herded his uncle's sheep and goats. Sometimes, he earned a few pennies by carrying loads of pottery to the market. Although he had a thirst for learning, there were no schools in the village to satisfy this desire. So, at the age of 12, Juárez decided to seek his fortune in the city of Oaxaca.

A Thirst for Education

When Juárez showed up on the doorstep of the Maza house in Oaxaca, the family was delighted to meet the thin, young boy. There was always room for one more person in the Maza household. He stayed with the Mazas during the winter months, helping out with chores.

Soon after his arrival, Juárez met a man who would help change his life. Don Antonio Salanueva was a good friend of the Mazas. He was a broad-minded man who had a vast library in his house. He was looking for a young person who would keep his house clean.

The boy deeply impressed Salanueva. Juárez was not only a hard worker, but he was also eager to learn. Even after a full day of work, he had the energy to study.

Salanueva was dedicated to the education of young people. Unlike many Criollos (kree-OH-yohs), he did not look down on Indios and Mestizos. Criollos were Spaniards born in Mexico and were the ruling class of the country. Many Criollos believed that Indios and Mestizos were not worth educating. Salanueva, however, immediately put the young Juárez into an elementary school with a good reputation. Juárez was excited at this opportunity.

However, his first day of school quickly discouraged him. On this first day, Juárez showed up at his classroom. A small group of well-dressed students sat at neat desks, their books piled in front of them. The teacher took one look at Juárez, pointed at a room in the back, and said, "You belong in there. This room is for Criollos."

The back room, Juárez found, was filled with poor Indio and Mestizo boys. These boys had no desks and no books. They sat crowded together on benches.

Juárez saw that the Criollos were carefully taught and treated with great respect. The Indio and Mestizo students were given little attention and treated harshly. Later in life, Juárez was still angry about this experience. "After some time in the fourth class, I could still hardly write at all," he remembered.

The proud Juárez could not accept this injustice. He decided to educate himself. He left the school and worked hard on his own to learn Spanish. After mastering the alphabet, he started reading simple books. Soon, he was reading all the books in Salanueva's library. His progress was so rapid that in 1821, he was accepted to a school that trained priests.

Here, he was well treated, and he advanced quickly. He not only learned to speak and write Spanish, he learned Latin as well. When he was 21, he went to another school to study religion, physics, philosophy, and church law. In 1831, when he was 25, he graduated and took a job with a lawyer. In a few years, he opened a small law office in the poorest part of Oaxaca.

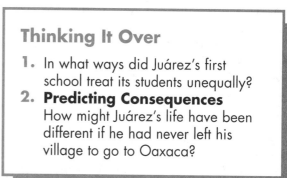

Thinking It Over

1. In what ways did Juárez's first school treat its students unequally?
2. **Predicting Consequences** How might Juárez's life have been different if he had never left his village to go to Oaxaca?

Active Learning: Create a timeline with the date 1800 on the left and 1880 on the right. At equal spaces along the line, put in the dates 1810, 1820, 1830, and so on. Section 1 covers the period from 1806 to 1831. Write the major events you have read about in Benito Juárez's life at the appropriate places on the timeline.

2 "I Am a Son of the People"

As a young man, Benito Juárez would always remember the way Mexico's justice system favored the wealthy over the poor.

In 1831, when Juárez began to practice law, Mexico had been independent from Spain for only 10 years. Mexico was a very rich country. During Juárez's youth, it extended far into what is today the southwestern United States. Much of its land was very fertile. Its mines produced one half of the world's silver.

Yet, most Mexicans were desperately poor and illiterate, which meant they were unable to read and write. Mexico's Indios and Mestizos had almost no power. The country was ruled by a small group of wealthy Criollos. This tiny group controlled the best land and the valuable mines. The gap between Mexico's rich and poor was vast.

The Roman Catholic Church had enormous power in Mexico. It was far more wealthy and powerful than the Mexican government. Many priests worked hard to improve conditions. However, some Church leaders worked against **reforms**, or improvements. They believed these reforms would weaken their power.

Revolving Door Government

When Mexico won independence from Spain in 1821, it set up a system that appeared democratic. But people were not familiar with how a democracy should work. Under Spanish rule, Mexico had not been a democracy. It also had very little experience governing itself. As a result, power struggles soon erupted between rival groups.

In the 40 years after Mexico became a republic, one leader after another seized power. In those 40 years, 56 governments came and went. General Antonio Lopez de Santa Anna, for example, seized power at least six times between 1832 and 1855.

For years, control of the Mexican government swung between two parties, the **Liberals** and the **Conservatives**. Conservatives wanted to preserve the power structure and the influence of the Catholic Church. They viewed freedom of speech and of the press as a threat to law and order. Liberals, on the other hand, called for rapid reform. They wanted to reduce the power of the Church over education and break up its vast estates.

Besides the divisions among Mexicans, the country also faced threats from the outside. During these years, Mexico suffered two terrible losses. In 1836, Mexico lost Texas to settlers who set up their own republic. Ten years later, the United States declared war on Mexico. The war ended in a complete U.S. victory. Mexico was forced to give up almost half its territory. This land now makes up all or part of seven U.S. states. The Mexican American War left Mexico with a feeling of bitterness toward the United States.

Fighting the Power of Privilege

As a young lawyer, Benito Juárez quickly gained a reputation as a defender of the poor. One day in 1835, a group of Zapotec Indios came to Juárez's office. The Zapotecs were nervous. They had never visited such an educated person. Juárez put them at ease and listened carefully to their complaint. A landowning priest was making them work at a wage so low that they could not survive. Could the lawyer do anything for them?

In those days in Mexico, cases involving priests were not tried in a government court. They were tried in a court run by the Church. These courts hardly ever ruled against priests. However, Juárez agreed to take the case without charge. He argued the case so well that the Church court agreed that the Indios had been wronged. The court suspended the priest and ordered that the peasants be paid.

This was not the end of the story, however. Two weeks after the court decision, a new Conservative government seized power. A stricter Church court reversed the order and had the Indios arrested. It also got an arrest warrant against Juárez. In the middle of the night, Juárez was pulled from his bed and hauled off to jail. He spent nine days in a filthy jail cell.

These nine days were a turning point for Juárez. He realized that Mexicans would never be treated equally as long as the wealthy had special privileges. As he later wrote, he decided to devote his life "to work constantly for the destruction of the evil power of the privileged class."

Demanding Honesty

Juárez became widely known in southern Mexico as a tough-minded and fiercely honest lawyer. He entered politics and was elected to a number of local positions. He worked to promote important reforms. He helped build roads around the city of Oaxaca and worked to improve the city's sanitation. Later he became a judge. In 1843, he was elected to the national congress in Mexico City.

In 1847, Juárez became governor of the Mexican state of Oaxaca. In those days, many officials accepted bribes and made fortunes. But the people respected Juárez because he was honest. He also demanded honesty from those who worked in his office. He fired officials who had gotten their jobs through important relatives or friends. In their place, Juárez gave jobs to able and hardworking people — no matter what their political views.

Not surprisingly, Juárez was very popular. A year later, he was elected to a second term. He made a speech to mark his **inauguration**, the formal beginning of his term. He said:

I am a son of the people. I shall not forget them. On the contrary, I shall provide for their education, and see that they grow and make a future for themselves.

Juárez kept his promise not to forget the people. As governor, he built several hundred schools. To fight poverty, he had roads built so that the people could get their crops to market. When an **epidemic**, a rapidly spreading disease, broke out in the mountains, he began a program of **vaccinations**. Vaccination is the process of giving medicines to people to prevent a serious disease.

Unfortunately, the vaccinations did not come until the disease was well under way. Many people died, including Juárez's two-year-old daughter, Guadalupe.

Juárez was concerned with improving life for all the people in the state. His large building projects helped make the economy stronger. These projects increased trade and reduced the state debt. They won Juárez support from different classes of Mexicans, not just the poor.

A Good Book to Read

Benito Juárez by Dennis Wepner, Chelsea House Publishers, New York, 1986.

Benito Juárez lived during the time when Mexico was emerging from three centuries as a Spanish colony. The story of Juárez's life is also a story of how Mexico became a modern nation. *Benito Juárez* is a fascinating story of the great Indio leader who led Mexico on the path to social reform and justice.

Exile in the United States

As a leading Liberal, Juárez fought for reforms that would bring the ideals of democratic government to Mexico. However, reforms were difficult because the country was headed toward a civil war. These were dangerous times for Liberals, and Juárez survived an assassination attempt. In 1853, he was arrested by Conservative troops and banished from the country. He went to New Orleans, Louisiana.

Like most Mexicans, Juárez resented the way the United States had taken Mexico's land. However, he respected the U.S. system of government. The United States was the model he looked to for building a democratic government in Mexico.

His life in the United States was difficult. Juárez spoke no English and could not earn a living as a lawyer. Instead, he worked as a cigar-roller and fished for his meals in the Mississippi River. During this period, he came down with a serious disease and almost died. But his will to live was strong, and he recovered.

Juárez never gave up hope of freeing his country from the Conservatives. He followed events in Mexico with keen interest. In 1855, he heard that fighting had broken out in Mexico and decided to return. Since he had no money, he worked his way back as a sailor, loading coal into the ship's engines. He arrived in Acapulco penniless and dressed in a ragged coat. There he joined a rebel force and helped bring down the Conservative government of Santa Anna.

Later that year, Santa Anna fled Mexico for Cuba. Juárez became Minister of Justice in the new Liberal government. Juárez was eager to reform the living conditions of the poor. Under his leadership, the reformers passed laws that reduced the wealth and power of the Church and the army. These laws called for some Church estates to be sold and divided among Indios.

In 1857, the Liberals created a new constitution. For the first time, it gave Mexicans a bill of rights. Under this bill of rights, Mexicans were guaranteed freedom of speech and of the press. They were also guaranteed equality before the law. Juárez's ideas for democratic reforms were finally put into practice.

The War of the Reform

The new constitution outraged Conservatives. Leaders of the Church threatened to deny religious rites to anyone who swore loyalty to the new constitution. Other Conservatives began training for war and built up supplies of arms. Conservatives called on Mexicans to resist the new constitution.

In 1858, civil war broke out. A civil war is fighting between citizens of the same country. Mexico's civil war was called the War of the Reform.

Early in the war, an army led by the landowners seized Mexico City. From town to town, Conservatives hunted for Juárez and killed many of his followers. Juárez escaped with a few followers and a copy of the constitution. His band traveled at night and slept in the fields during the day. At one point, they were captured and came within a hair of being shot before they managed to escape.

At last they reached the city of Veracruz on the east coast. For a time, Juárez set up a government in Veracruz. However, the situation was grim. Juárez was the head of a government without a capital city, without funds, and without an army. A Veracruz newspaper made fun of him: "A little Indian by the name of Juárez, who calls himself president of Mexico, has arrived in this city."

Juárez did not give up hope. Supporters began reaching Veracruz and were trained for battle. One by one, Juárez's army conquered the important towns and cities of Mexico. Finally, in January of 1861, Juárez led his victorious soldiers back into Mexico City.

On June 11, 1861, Juárez was elected president of Mexico. He was the first Indio to rule over Mexico since the Spanish conquest of the Aztecs.

Thinking It Over

1. On what issues did the Conservatives and Liberals disagree?
2. **Determining Cause and Effect** (a) What was the cause of the new constitution in Mexico? (b) What was the effect?

Active Learning: This section describes events in Benito Juárez's life between 1831 and 1861. It was an historic period in Mexico. Make a list of some of these events and place the most important ones on your timeline.

3 The French Threat

The War of the Reform lasted almost three years. The fighting left the Mexican economy in ruins. The cost of the war drained the national treasury. There was not even enough money to pay the soldiers who had fought in the war. Bands of former soldiers from both sides roamed the country burning, looting, and killing.

During the war, Mexico had been forced to borrow large amounts of money from foreign countries. Unfortunately, there was no money to pay back these debts. Mexico tried to borrow money from the United States, but President James Buchanan was not interested in giving the loan. Then Abraham Lincoln was elected president. Juárez received Lincoln's promise. Lincoln pledged "to do everything in my power to deal justly with Mexico." But Lincoln also said that with the outbreak of the U.S. Civil War, the United States was fighting for its own survival. At this point, it could spare no aid.

Faced with an empty treasury six months after regaining power, Juárez announced that Mexico would not repay the foreign powers for a period of two years.

With Juárez's announcement, the Emperor of France, Napoleon III, saw an opportunity to create an empire in Mexico. He was encouraged by Mexico's Conservatives, who were eager to regain power from the Liberals. In late 1861, Napoleon sent troops to Mexico to collect the money owed to France.

As a Liberal, Juárez fought for democratic reform. He believed in creating a less powerful government and a strong economy.

Cinco de Mayo

The French army was then one of the most powerful forces in the world. Landing at Veracruz, the French began to move inland. Several thousand French troops marched on Mexico City. The Mexican forces built their defenses at the city of Puebla and waited for the French. The French general, believing that Puebla would fall within a few days, boldly announced:

We are so superior to the Mexicans in race, in organization, in discipline, in morality, and in refinement, that as of this moment, at the head of our 6,000 valiant soldiers, I am the master of Mexico.

Juárez responded:

We must now prove to France and to the entire world that we are worthy to be free.

And this they did. The Mexicans were greatly outnumbered. Poorly trained, they faced one of the best-trained armies in the world. However, they turned back the French attack. Then they themselves attacked and scattered the French.

The Mexican victory at Puebla took place in 1862, on the fifth of May, or cinco de mayo. With this battle, Mexico showed the world that it could defend itself from foreign interference. Every year on that date, Mexicans hold a grand celebration called cinco de mayo. In the United States, Mexican Americans also celebrate cinco de mayo. In Los Angeles, for example, a three-day fiesta is held around the city's oldest street, Olvera Street. People come to remember the day on which a small force of Mexicans defeated the powerful armies of the French.

When the Mexican army defeated the French at Puebla, Mexico proved that it could protect itself from foreign invasion.

A French Emperor of Mexico

A year after his defeat at Puebla, Napoleon sent a huge army to Mexico. Facing approximately 30,000 French soldiers, the small Mexican army could not hold out long. In 1863, the French defeated the Mexicans, drove Juárez into the mountains, and took over Mexico City.

Napoleon chose an Austrian noble named Maximilian to rule Mexico. With Conservative support, Maximilian was proclaimed Emperor of Mexico. Maximilian wanted to help Mexico develop its economy. He also admired Juárez. However, he had no real idea of the responsibilities he had taken on. Maximilian told the French that he did not want to rule unless the Mexican people really wanted him. When he arrived in Mexico in 1864, he found streets lined with crowds of cheering people. He did not realize that French soldiers had forced the Mexican people to stage this welcome.

Juárez and his followers continued to resist foreign rule. In the north, they moved from city to city just one step ahead of the French. As always, Juárez kept up his courage. At one point, he was escaping in a carriage with bullets whizzing all around. Someone cried out for the coachman to push the horses to a gallop. Juárez said no. He declared, "The president of the republic does not run."

By 1865, the situation had changed in Juárez's favor. With the end of the U.S. Civil War, the United States was ready to take strong action against the French. The United States feared that a powerful French army could also be a threat to the United States, and perhaps try to take back the Louisiana territory.

In 1865, the U.S. government demanded that the French leave Mexico. To back up the threat, the United States sent 100,000 troops under General Philip Sheridan to the Texas border. It also provided arms and supplies to the Mexicans and sent troops to join Juárez's army.

A discouraged Napoleon decided to bring the French troops home. Maximilian could have left with them, but he chose to stay.

With the departure of the French, Maximilian was helpless. He had no army to hold back the forces of Juárez. In May 1867, Juárez's army captured Maximilian. After a trial, Maximilian was sentenced to death. Juárez received many requests for mercy and considered them carefully. In the end, he turned them down. He feared that Mexican opponents would use Maximilian to fight against democracy. Juárez said to one woman:

If all the kings and queens of Europe were at your side, I could not spare his life. It is not I who take it away. It is my people and the law.

On June 19, 1867, Maximilian and two Mexican generals who had supported him were executed.

Unchallenged Leader

With the defeat of the French, Juárez came back in triumph to Mexico City and ruled as president. In his last years, he passed laws calling for many reforms. He started schools to educate Indio

After the French victory in 1863, Napoleon sent Austrian noble, Maximilian, to rule Mexico. Three years after the nobleman's arrival, Benito Juárez's forces defeated the French and executed Maximilian. This painting shows the execution of Maximilian and two Mexican generals who supported him.

children and reduced the size of the army. He made laws to further reduce the power of the Church. He built railroads and tried to improve the country's finances.

Because he focused on these problems, Juárez was unable to give out much land to the people who most needed it. On July 18, 1872, before he had a chance to carry out many reforms, the great leader suffered a heart attack and died.

Building a Nation

Benito Juárez devoted his life to the struggle for justice and democracy in Mexico. All his life, he fought against great odds. Born into deep poverty and an orphan, he managed to educate himself. Juárez rose to power at a time when his country was split by civil war. His energy and fairness strengthened the cause of democracy in Mexico.

Juárez died at the height of his powers — before his work was done. His death meant that the reforms he dreamed of would not be achieved in his lifetime. Mexico would not make progress in closing the gap between wealth and poverty for another half-century.

Active Learning: This section describes events in Mexico from the end of the War of the Reform to the death of Juárez. Put the key events on your timeline.

Thinking It Over

1. What happened on the fifth of May, or cinco de mayo, in 1862?
2. **Analyzing Primary Sources** Study the comments made by the French general and by Juárez before the battle on cinco de mayo on pages 33–34. How could each man's attitude have affected the outcome of the battle?

This painting by Mexican muralist José Clemente Orozco commemorates the return of Benito Juárez to Mexico City. Orozco captured the admiration and love Mexicans have for Juárez. Based on what you have read in this case study, why do you think Juárez is Mexico's best-loved leader?

GOING TO THE SOURCE

Benito Juárez Stands Up for Indios

As a young lawyer, Benito Juárez took many cases in which he defended poor people. None made more of an impression on him than the case of the Zapotec farmers discussed in the case study. (See pages 30–31.) They had complained to Juárez that a parish priest was taking advantage of them. Both the Indios and Juárez were arrested for bringing the issue to court. Later in life, Juárez wrote:

I left my teaching job and went to the town of Miahuatlán (mee-ah-wha-TLAN), where the prisoners were, in order to liberate [free] them. I presented myself to the judge. I asked him to inform me of the nature of the case against the prisoners. He answered that he could tell me nothing because the case was kept secret. I told him that on the following day, I would present him a petition [appeal] forcing him to answer me in writing.

The following day, I presented my petition. The judge received me coldly and demanded to know with what power was I acting. I answered that I was speaking in defense of poor people everywhere. He turned down my request. So the doors of justice remained closed to those unhappy ones who suffered in prison without having committed any offense, only because they had complained of the oppressions. . . .

The judge in the capital came to my house at midnight and took me to the jail without giving me any more reason than that he had received an order to take me prisoner.

So false was the charge made against me and so clear the injustice that I believed it certain that the Court to which I appealed would give immediate orders to set me at liberty. However, I was mistaken. For it was only after nine days that it freed me on bail.

These blows that I suffered, and that almost daily I saw suffered by the unprotected, showed me most clearly that society would never be happy while the privileged classes were allied with the public powers. It confirmed me in my determination to work unceasingly [without stopping] to destroy the evil power of the privileged classes.

From Benito Juárez, *Notes to My Children*,
quoted in *Viva Juárez!*, by Charles Allen Smart,
Lippincott, 1963, p. 67.

1. What reason did the judge give for taking Juárez to jail?
2. **Understanding Consequences** What were the short-term consequences of the Zapotec case for Juárez? What were the long-term consequences?

Case Study Review

Identifying Main Ideas

1. How did Juárez overcome the prejudice he faced in school?
2. What were some differences between Mexico's Liberals and Conservatives?
3. What were some of the reforms that Juárez fought for in Mexico?

Working Together

Form a small group. Write at least five newspaper headlines about important events in Mexican history that are covered in this case study. Then choose one headline and write a brief article to accompany it. You may also wish to draw an illustration for your article.

Active Learning

Creating a Timeline Review the timeline of events in Mexico from 1800 to 1880 that you created as you read this case study. Now, use a textbook about U.S. history to add to your timeline the events that happened in the United States during this same period. Use a different color pencil, pen, or marker to show the U.S. events. You may wish to transfer the information to a larger sheet of paper and present your work to the class.

Lessons for Today

When the situation appeared bleakest, Juárez always remained unshakable in his beliefs. During the French invasions, he wrote, "Forty-five thousand French troops in the country now. All mouths for the French to pay and feed. No wonder the French are grumbling more loudly about the expense of this war. I think that before long, my friends, our tide will begin to turn. We will be in Mexico City again one of these days." What beliefs do you feel strongly about? How can faith in your beliefs help you through a difficult time?

What Might You Have Done?

It is 1861. Mexico owes Britain, France, and Spain a large amount of money after its civil war. Yet it has almost no money to repay the European nations. The three nations are threatening to invade if they are not repaid. You are an advisor to Benito Juárez, president of Mexico. What would you advise him to do? Why?

During the time that Benito Juárez was struggling against the French in Mexico, Abraham Lincoln became President of the United States. On the surface, Lincoln and Juárez appear to have little in common.

Lincoln was a tall Anglo born in Kentucky. At six foot four inches, he towered over other Americans of his time. Juárez was a short Indio, who was barely five feet tall. He was born in a tiny mountain village where people had little contact with the outside world. Yet the two had a number of things in common.

- Both men were born into deep poverty.
- Both lost parents at an early age.
- Against all odds, both managed to educate themselves and pull themselves out of poverty.
- Both rose to power at a time when their countries were divided by civil war.
- Their greatest accomplishment was attacking injustice.
- Both were beloved political figures of their country.

Below is a Venn diagram. It is used to help compare and contrast people and issues. Copy the diagram into your notebook. In the overlapping part of the circles, write down all the things Lincoln and Juárez had in common. In the parts that do not overlap, write down what was unique about each leader. Use your library to find a biography of Lincoln to help you with the task. Then write an essay comparing the two men.

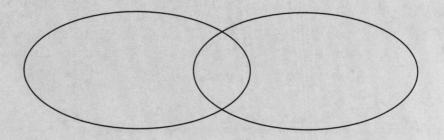

EMILIANO ZAPATA: HERO OF THE MEXICAN REVOLUTION

Emiliano Zapata, the great champion of justice during the Mexican Revolution, is shown in a painting by the Mexican artist, Diego Rivera.

CRITICAL QUESTIONS

■ How did Emiliano Zapata become a leading symbol of Mexico's fight for justice for all?

■ How did the Mexican Revolution affect the lives of Mexicans?

TERMS TO KNOW

■ ejido   ■ guerrilla

■ haciendas   ■ deported

■ Zapatistas   ■ defect

ACTIVE LEARNING

A biography is the story of a person's life. In this section, you will read about the life of Emiliano Zapata, a hero of the Mexican Revolution. After you have read the case study, you will write a one- or two-page biography that explains why Zapata's life story is important to people today. Look for the Active Learning hint boxes throughout the case study. They will help you write the biography.

All his life, Emiliano Zapata would never forget the few days he spent training the horses of the very rich landowner, Don Ignacio Torre y Mier. To his horror, Zapata saw that Don Ignacio's horses lived in better conditions than did peasants back in Zapata's home state of Morelos.

He did not last in the job very long. Disgusted with the luxury of the rich, Zapata returned to his home village. He was determined to destroy the wealth of the landowning families.

This determination led Zapata to become one of Mexico's greatest champions of the poor and one of its greatest fighters for justice for all Mexicans. In 1994, rebels in the Mexican state of Chiapas showed their respect for him. They said:

Zapata will continue to live as long as people believe that they have a right to govern themselves according to their deeply held beliefs.

Emiliano Zapata was a man who achieved tremendous power in Mexico, yet he never sought that power. He died without reaching his goal, yet his life is an inspiration to people all over the world who struggle for justice.

1 Defender of the Poor

In 1879, around the time Zapata was born, conditions had changed little in Mexico since 1821, the year of independence. Most Mexicans remained poor farmers, growing beans and corn and raising livestock. In many villages, the farm land was owned and worked by the village as a group, called the **ejido** (eh-HEE-doh), rather than by individual farmers. The ejido allowed the farmers to pool their resources and work the land more efficiently.

This way of life began to change dramatically in the last years of the 1800s. Large ranches, called **haciendas** (ah-see-EHN-dahs), began to take over the land.

By selling off the resources of the land, the owners of the haciendas became fabulously wealthy. In Morelos, just south of Mexico City, sugar growing became an important industry. In a few years, Morelos became the world's third largest sugar-producing area.

Growing sugar cane was so profitable that the wealthy landowners began to look for more land on which to grow it. Often they simply seized land from the villages. Many times, they bribed judges to take land from the ejidos. Many Indios who protested were killed, shipped off to work camps, or drafted into the army. The farmers who stayed were forced to work on the haciendas.

Mexican villagers lost their land to hacienda owners. This painting by Diego Rivera shows how many of Mexico's Indios labored in harsh conditions to make the hacienda owners extremely wealthy.

The Díaz Years

In 1876, Porfirio Díaz seized control of the government. He ruled Mexico for the next 35 years. On the surface, the Díaz years were a time of peace and prosperity. The Mexican economy grew strong as investors built mines, oil wells, and railroads. Vast sums of foreign money poured into Mexico. Mexico City became one of the most beautiful and modern capitals in the world.

Much of the new money came from the United States. Many wealthy Americans put their money into Mexican railroads, mines, and oil wells. It was important to these investors that Mexico have peace and stability.

Land of Wealth and Poverty

For most Mexicans, the years of Díaz's rule were times of despair and empty stomachs. Few Mexicans benefited from the new prosperity. The benefits went chiefly to the well-to-do.

About 96 percent of rural families did not own land in 1910. Many of these families were deeply in debt to hacienda owners. This situation limited their freedom and their ability to make better lives for themselves. By law, they had to remain on the estates as long as they owed money to the owner.

Living under these conditions, Mexico's poor were oppressed. They needed a leader who would challenge the power of the wealthy.

Seeds of Revolt

Emiliano Zapata was born to Mestizo peasants, probably in 1879. Zapata himself was not sure of the date. Unlike most peasant families, Zapata's family was not desperately poor. His father trained and sold horses.

However, both his parents died when Zapata was 17, and he was forced to care for his younger brothers and sisters. In 1897, he was arrested for taking part in a protest by peasants of his village who had lost their lands to an hacienda owner. With the help of a brother, Zapata escaped and hid in the mountains for a year. When the soldiers stopped looking for him, he returned to his village.

Zapata became fairly prosperous in his town. He farmed a small piece of land and raised horses. He earned extra money by organizing pack trains of mules that took goods from one town to another. For a time, he worked as a rodeo trick rider.

Zapata was determined to defend his village's land rights. Villagers respected Zapata as a man of courage and honesty. In 1909, the elders of his village elected him president of the board of defense for their village. This was an Indio custom.

However, this position made him a serious troublemaker in the eyes of the authorities. One way of dealing with troublemakers was to draft them into the army. Zapata was drafted and served for six months. When the local landowner, Don Ignacio, found out that Zapata was in the army, he requested that Zapata be assigned to him. The young Zapata was discharged to train Don Ignacio's horses in Mexico City.

Zapata disliked the city and returned to his village in 1910. He again challenged the power of the landowners. When his arguments got no results, Zapata and a group of peasants occupied by force land that had been taken from the peasants. They distributed this land among themselves.

Thinking It Over

1. How did the growth of sugar plantations in Morelos affect land ownership in the state?
2. **Drawing Conclusions** Why do you suppose someone who is considered a troublemaker would be drafted into the army?

2 The Mexican Revolution

The year 1910 was a turning point in Mexican history. September 16 marked the 100th anniversary of Mexico's independence movement. Díaz held an elaborate celebration with fireworks, banquets, and parades. The government spent more money on the celebration than on the entire education budget for the year.

Earlier that year, a number of rebellions against Díaz's rule had broken out all over Mexico. The rebels soon accepted the leadership of a man named Francisco Madero. Later in the year, Díaz was forced to resign.

Unfortunately, once Díaz was gone, the revolutionary ranks divided. Revolutionaries are people who participate in a revolution. For the next few years, the country was in an uproar as army fought army for control of Mexico. Governments and alliances came and went. Alliances are agreements between groups to support one other.

In his 16 months in office, Madero faced six different major rebellions. In 1913, he was murdered by a general named Victoriano Huerta. In 1914, Huerta was forced out of office by a leader named Venustiano Carranza. Carranza's followers then split. Civil war broke out among the leaders. For two years, a number of other rivals fought Carranza for power.

"Join Me!"

When fighting first broke out in 1910, Emiliano Zapata was barely known outside his village. When he heard of the uprising, Zapata organized a band of 80 armed men. Within weeks, his forces had seized a number of haciendas. In March 1911, Zapata's tiny force took the city of Cuautla (KWOW-tluh). Then, with 5,000 soldiers, he entered Cuernavaca, capital of the state of Morelos. As Zapata's successes continued, his power grew, and peasants flocked to join him. Soon, Zapata was commanding a small army.

The people of Morelos felt a special bond with Zapata. He spoke the local Indio language Náhuatl (NAH-what-ahl) to recruit more followers. Late in her life, a women remembered the day that Zapata rode into her village. She said:

> When he entered the village, all of his men wore white clothes. All of these men spoke Náhuatl, almost as we spoke it. Señor Zapata also spoke it, and as a result when those men came into my village, everyone understood them. Señor Zapata went to the front of his men and spoke to all the people of the village in Náhuatl.

> "Join me," Señor Zapata said. "I rose up in arms and I bring my countrymen. I want everyone to have his piece of land so that he can plant and harvest corn, beans, and other crops. Are you ready to join us?"

Women Answer the Call

Many women responded to Zapata's call to arms. Some of these women became officers in his army. Maria Chavarria, for example, was a colonel in Zapata's forces.

In the town of Puente de Ixtla, the women of the village took up arms and formed their own military unit. This unit became an important part of Zapata's army.

In all of Mexico, women played an important role in the revolutionary armies. Some served as spies. Thousands of women became

This picture from 1911 shows Mexican peasants, both women and men, marching off to battle. Thousands of Mexican women became soldaderas, women soldiers, and fought to replace the old unfair government with one that would bring justice to all Mexicans.

soldaderas (SOHL-dah-DEH-rahs), or women soldiers, who marched and fought with the army.

Land and Liberty

When the Mexican Revolution first broke out, Zapata pledged loyalty to Madero. He expected the new leader to restore village rights to the land. Zapata was not interested in national power. He was focused on problems in Morelos. Under the banner *"Tierra y Libertad"* ("Land and Liberty"), the **Zapatistas**, the followers of Zapata, continued to seize estates in Morelos.

In Mexico City, however, the problems looked different. Madero and the others had no intention of breaking up the big estates. They were mostly concerned with bringing order to Mexico. They saw the armed bands such as the Zapatistas as bandits. When Madero refused to break up the estates, Zapata called him a traitor and began seizing more estates.

The Plan of Ayala

Zapata's activities frightened the leaders of the new Mexican government. They worried about his growing power. In September 1911, they sent an army to deal with Zapata. The army carried out acts of brutality against villages in Morelos. It killed innocent villagers, destroyed their homes, and forced many of them into hiding in the mountains.

From their hiding place, Zapata and his followers drew up a document known as the Plan of Ayala. Stolen lands, the document stated, would be taken away from the landowners and returned to the villagers. Hacienda owners who agreed to the plan would lose one third of their land. However, owners who refused to accept this plan would lose *all* their land. The Plan of Ayala stated:

> *The land, woods, and water that the landlords or bosses have taken will be immediately restored to the villages or citizens who hold title to them.*

Once the federal army had left, the people of Morelos emerged from the mountains. When they saw the smoking ruins of their villages, many joined Zapata's forces.

The Zapatistas Strike Back

Emiliano Zapata and his followers fought hard to reclaim land from the wealthy and win rights for the poor. They lived in violent times, times in which both sides were ruthless. During the revolution, both the Zapatistas and the federal army ordered executions and burned property.

Zapata's forces were outraged by the brutality that Mexican peasants had faced over the centuries. They took their anger out on the wealthy landowners. Zapata's soldiers swooped down on haciendas. If an owner of an hacienda surrendered, he escaped with his life. However, if an hacienda owner held out, Zapata's forces would destroy the hacienda, burn buildings and crops, and shoot the owner and managers.

The owners of sugar plantations were the first to feel the resentment of the Zapatistas. Sugar was the main source of wealth in Morelos. Eager to grow more sugar, the landowners had stolen peasant lands. Because much of Morelos planted only sugar cane, there was nothing to eat during lean winters. Children who ate only sugar cane did not survive these winters. Therefore, the Zapatistas were particularly angry at the sugar growers. The Zapatistas also captured towns, blew up railroad bridges, and cut telegraph wires.

The United States Takes Sides

Morelos was only one scene of the Mexican Revolution. In the north, Francisco (Pancho) Villa formed his own army and began advancing toward Mexico City. Villa was a poor man with no military training. However, he was very intelligent and proved to be an able leader. He built his army into a superb **guerrilla** force. Guerrillas fight from cover and stage hit-and-run raids. Villa defeated much larger armies sent against him and, like Zapata, began seizing large estates.

By now, Huerta had seized power and murdered Madero. All this violence troubled the United States. The U.S. government worried that the fighting would harm U.S. properties in Mexico. The United States thought that a new leader would bring stability to Mexico. It decided to support Venustiano Carranza. It believed that Carranza would be friendlier to U.S. interests.

The United States also decided to take action. In April 1914, it seized the port of Veracruz. The excuse for the seizure was that U.S. sailors had been insulted in an incident in the city of Tampico. The real reason for seizing the port was to prevent arms from reaching Huerta.

U.S. control of Veracruz dealt a major blow to Huerta. Without the new arms, Huerta was unable to challenge the growing forces that were against him. Huerta was forced out of power, and Carranza took over.

However, in other ways, the seizure backfired. It caused a storm of protest in Mexico. The Mexican people were outraged by the seizure. As a result, Carranza had to take a strong stand against U.S. interference.

Seizing Mexico City

Like the other leaders of Mexico before him, Carranza had no interest in land reform. So Zapata formed an alliance with Pancho Villa. These two leaders promised to fight together until they had defeated Carranza. Their armies marched on Mexico City. Carranza fled, and about 50,000 peasant-soldiers from Zapata's and Villa's armies took over the capital. Zapata and Villa held a meeting in the city and posed for historic photographs.

For weeks, the people of Mexico City had feared what the peasant armies might do when

Carrying the banner of an independent Mexico, soldiers of the revolution entered the city of Tampico after driving out government forces in 1914. Soon the Federal forces would take the offensive against their chief enemies, Zapata and Villa.

they took over the city. What happened was in some ways a pleasant surprise. City dwellers watched in astonishment as Zapata's forces went from door to door asking for food and drink. There was little attacking and burning by Zapata's forces.

Zapata did not stay in Mexico City for long. Feeling uncomfortable in the city, he left it and returned to Morelos. "The city is full of sidewalks and I keep falling off of them," he joked.

A Rural Movement

Zapata's roots were in the countryside, and his movement remained a rural movement. His reforms were almost entirely directed toward Mexico's peasant farmers. He redistributed lands, established schools, and developed rural industries.

Zapata created commissions to distribute the land. He spent much time supervising their work to be sure they were fair. He also established a bank to lend money to peasants.

The U.S. Pursues Villa

Unlike Zapata, Pancho Villa sought to lead all of Mexico. However, he could not defeat the forces against him. In a series of battles in April 1915, Villa was attacked by forces loyal to Carranza. In the battle of Celaya, Villa unleashed his poorly equipped army against Carranza's forces, which had machine guns. Again and again, the Villa forces attacked. Each time they were driven back. When the battle was over, 5,000 of Villa's troops lay dead on the battlefield. Villa was driven north with only a tiny band of supporters. Soon he was in hiding in the mountains.

Villa was angry that the United States had backed Carranza instead of himself. In March 1916, Villa decided to attack the Americans.

Just before dawn on March 9, Villa's forces entered the town of Columbus, New Mexico. For the next two hours, Villa's forces controlled the town. When they withdrew, 18 Americans were dead and the town was burned. To catch Villa, the U.S. government sent 6,000 men under General John J. Pershing into Mexico.

For 11 months, Pershing's forces searched for Villa. They never found him. Villa always managed to stay one step ahead of the Americans. After the U.S. force left Mexico, Villa retired to his ranch in the north. There he worked hard to improve conditions among the peasants on his land. He built schools and provided peasants with loans. However, he never got the chance to finish his reforms. In 1923, he was murdered by political opponents.

The Zimmermann Telegram

The Pershing invasion further soured relations between Mexico and the United States. Mexicans were outraged that the United States had invaded their country again. Had Mexico not been so divided, the two countries might have gone to war.

In addition, World War I was underway in Europe. The United States and Mexico watched the development of the war in Europe with growing concern. Soon, another incident would add to the bad feelings between the United States and Mexico.

In early 1917, the United States had not yet entered World War I. However, it was only a matter of months until the United States declared war on Germany. Meanwhile, Carranza received a strange proposal from a German government official, Arthur Zimmermann. If Mexico joined an alliance with Germany, Zimmermann said, Germany would return the territory that Mexico had lost in the Mexican American War. Mexicans were so angry at the United States that Carranza was tempted to

accept the offer. However, he realized that Germany had no power to defend Mexico in the event of a war with the United States.

When the Zimmermann telegram became known, it caused outrage in the United States. In April 1917, the United States declared war against Germany. Although Mexico did not join the war, the United States remained suspicious of its neighbor. Relations between the United States and Mexico were at a low point. Discrimination against Mexican Americans also increased. Many Anglos considered anyone of Mexican heritage to be a potential enemy.

Thinking It Over

1. How did Pancho Villa contribute to improving the lives of villagers in the north of Mexico?
2. **Comparing** How did Zapata's and Villa's goals for the revolution differ?

Active Learning: For your biography of Zapata, take notes on his accomplishments during the Mexican Revolution.

3 Ambush!

With the defeat of Pancho Villa, Carranza's generals turned their attention to Zapata. During his life, Zapata was much loved by the villagers of Mexico. He won their trust with his fairness. He impressed them with his riding ability and sense of style. Zapata always took care to dress neatly. He often wore a dark suit sewn with silver medals, silver spurs, a silk handkerchief

Pancho Villa, at center, was a poor man with no military training. However, he proved to be an able military leader who built his army into a superb guerrilla fighting force.

around his neck, and a large sombrero, or hat. As Zapata entered a village, he was greeted warmly by residents of all ages.

The more popular Zapata became, the more the Mexican government began to fear him. In June 1916, Carranza sent General Pablo Gonzalez to defeat Zapata.

With Zapata and his forces well hidden in the mountains, Gonzalez knew that the usual kind of warfare would not work. Instead, he waged war on the people of Morelos.

Gonzalez executed thousands of peasants and **deported**, or sent away, hundreds more. He burned every village he came across. He cut down forests and sent the wood back to Mexico City. He stripped hotels and public buildings of furniture and plumbing. The fighting in Morelos was among the worst of the entire revolution.

The Zapatistas responded with violence. They shot prisoners that they captured. In one case, they blew up a train and killed about 400 civilian passengers. Then Zapata retreated to the mountains to wait.

Gonzalez decided to set a trap for Zapata. He ordered Colonel Jesus Guajardo to pretend to **defect**, or switch sides. Guajardo wrote to Zapata and said he was prepared to take his 500 troops and all of their arms over to the Zapatista cause. He asked for a meeting with Zapata.

On April 10, 1919, Zapata rode with his bodyguards through the gates of an hacienda where Guajardo was staying. In the sunlit courtyard, Zapata saw over 600 men arranged as an honor guard. They raised their rifles as if to salute Zapata. Zapata smiled at the men and dismounted. He took several steps toward the house. Then someone gave an order to fire, and two quick shots were fired point blank into Zapata's body. He collapsed in the dust and died instantly. He was 39 years old.

Zapata's body was carried to Cuautla and dumped in the street as a warning to the peasants. Later he was put in a coffin. That night tearful peasants paraded past the coffin. However, after he was buried, his followers began hearing rumors that Zapata was not dead. Many followers believed that Zapata was hiding in the mountains, waiting to emerge and continue his struggle for the peasants of Mexico. (See *Going to the Source* on page 51.)

The Price of Revolution

Long before Zapata's death, important changes were underway in Mexico. There was a new constitution approved in 1917. It gave the government the power to distribute land to peasants. It recognized the rights of workers to form unions. The new constitution established the right to vote for all adult males. This constitution is still in force in Mexico.

Fighting went on in Mexico for many years. However, the changes brought about by the

A Good Movie to See

Viva Zapata, directed by Elia Kazan. Starring Marlon Brando and Anthony Quinn, 1952. 105 minutes.

This movie is almost half a century old, but it still crackles with drama. It stars the well-known actor Marlon Brando in the role of Emiliano Zapata. Anthony Quinn, the Mexican American actor, won an Academy Award for best supporting actor. See this movie and get caught up in the excitement.

Mexican Revolution did improve the lives of Mexicans. These changes came at a terrible price. Perhaps 1.5 million people were killed in the revolution. This was one out of every 10 people in the country! Few Mexican families were spared the loss of a loved one.

Many Mexicans attempted to flee the violence by coming to the United States. Between 1910 and 1920, thousands of Mexicans fled across the border. They came on foot, on horseback, in wagons, and on railroad trains. Most Mexican immigrants settled in the southwestern part of the United States. Many of them moved to the cities where they established large Mexican American communities.

Active Learning: To complete your biography of Zapata, take notes on his death and his long-term contributions to improving the lives of Mexican peasants.

The Legacy of Zapata

Of all the leaders of the Mexican Revolution, Emiliano Zapata is by far the most famous. Yet Zapata never achieved power outside the state of Morelos. He was committed to restoring to the poor farmers of Morelos the land that had been stolen from them.

This goal was achieved after his death. In the 1920s, Morelos saw extensive land reform. By 1927, four out of five farm families in Morelos owned land of their own.

Zapata's life became an inspiration for revolutions that would sweep the world in the 20th century. Earlier revolutions arose in the cities. After Zapata's death, peasant-based revolutions occurred in Africa, Asia, and Latin America. Zapata became a legend. His story was told in popular songs, poems, and in Mexican art.

In 1914, Zapata and Pancho Villa seized Mexico City. Zapata felt uncomfortable in the city and left it after a couple of days. While there, however, he posed for a picture with his leading advisors and bodyguards. Zapata is seated at center.

Revolutionaries are still inspired by Emiliano Zapata. On January 1, 1994, fighting broke out in the Mexican state of Chiapas. The rebels named themselves the Zapatista Army of National Liberation after Zapata, Mexico's great defender of peasant rights. In Chiapas, as in Morelos a century earlier, there were great natural riches. And as in Morelos, those riches benefited only a few. Using the same slogan Zapata had used— "Land and Liberty"—the rebels of Chiapas vowed to fight for peasant rights as the Zapatistas had done more than 85 years earlier.

Thinking It Over

1. What was Colonel Guajardo's plan to trap Zapata?
2. **Analyzing a Quote** Later in life, Zapata said, "It is better to live on your feet than to die on your knees." In your own words, what do you think Zapata meant? In what ways did Zapata live by this code?

GOING TO THE SOURCE

Zapata Rides Again

Many of Morelos's peasants could not believe that Zapata was dead. For many years after 1919, they would tell stories that Zapata had been seen on a white horse in the mountains. He would return, many believed, when he was needed again by the peasants. For them, he was too strong and too smart to die. Zapata continues to live on in folk stories and poems, such as this one.

Little star in the night
that rides the sky like a witch
where is our chief Zapata
who was the scourge [plague] of the rich?

Little flower of the fields
and valleys of Morelos, if they ask for Zapata,
say he's gone to try on halos.

Little bubbling brook,
what did that carnation say to you?
It says that our chief didn't die.
That Zapata's on his way to you.

Mexican corrida, or folk ballad

1. What is the meaning of this phrase: "if they ask for Zapata, say he's gone to try on halos"?
2. **Analyzing Poetry** How does this poem reflect the idea that Zapata waits in the mountains until he is needed by the Mexican people?

Case Study Review

Identifying Main Ideas

1. Why was Emiliano Zapata drafted into the Mexican army?
2. What was Zapata's main goal in the Mexican Revolution?
3. What rights did Mexicans gain with the constitution of 1917?

Working Together

Choose three or four classmates to work with. Conduct research on an outstanding Mexican other than Emiliano Zapata and Benito Juárez. Some possibilities include: Cuahtemoc, the last Aztec emperor; Frida Kahlo, the artist; Father Manuel Hidalgo, who led Mexico's independence struggle; and Lazaro Cárdinas, Mexican president. After you have done your research, prepare an oral presentation for the class.

Active Learning

Writing a Biography Review the notes you took as you were reading about Emiliano Zapata. Now write a one-or two-page biography that explains why Zapata's life story is important to people today. Include one or two paragraphs for each of the sections in the case study.

Lessons for Today

Emiliano Zapata is still remembered for his struggle for justice for all Mexicans. Think of another hero from the past who is still admired today. What did this hero fight for? How did this hero contribute to improving the lives of others? What do you think others can learn from the beliefs and experiences of this hero?

What Might You Have Done?

Imagine that you are a supporter of Emiliano Zapata as the Mexican Revolution is just breaking out in 1910. How would you advise him to carry out the goals of the Mexican Revolution and deal with other leaders?

CRITICAL THINKING

Comparing Points of View on the Mexican Revolution

Playing a Role

When you role play, you play the part of another person. You try to think like the person and communicate the person's ideas. Role-playing can help you better understand someone else's point of view.

People often view the same event or situation differently. A person's point of view depends largely on his or her particular interests. For example, a major snowstorm would make a store owner think about lost income because customers would stay at home. Store employees, however, may welcome the storm as an opportunity to take time off from work.

In the same way, people look at historical events from very different points of view. People who feel very strongly about an issue are often surprised to find out that a person who is on the opposite side can feel just as strongly. One of the most difficult tasks for a critical thinker is to try to "put yourself in the other person's shoes"—to try to look at events from a totally different point of view.

Form groups of four. Have each person in the group role play one of the following people:

- a landless peasant in the state of Morelos
- an American investor in Mexican railways
- a member of Mexico's central government in Mexico City
- a Mexican historian today

From the viewpoint of the role you are playing, think carefully about the following questions. Try to answer as the person you are playing would answer.

- What kind of a man is Emiliano Zapata?
- Is the Mexican Revolution good or bad?
- Should the United States intervene in Mexican affairs?

As a group, have a discussion in which you present and compare your individual points of view. Remember that you are each playing a role. Be sure everyone has a chance to speak.

MEXICAN AMERICANS DEFEND THE UNITED STATES

Proud to serve their country, these young Mexican American recruits line up to learn drills. They would soon be shipped overseas to fight in World War II.

CRITICAL QUESTIONS

- How have Mexican Americans contributed to the U.S. armed forces?
- How has Mexican American service in the armed forces helped to fight discrimination in the United States?

TERMS TO KNOW

- Patriots
- compromises
- cryptographers
- GI Bill

ACTIVE LEARNING

In this case study, you will read about the heroism of Mexican Americans who fought to defend the United States. At the end of the case study, you will choose one of the people you have read about. Then you will work with a partner to role play an interview with that person. Look for the Active Learning hint s to help you with your assignment.

The Japanese soldiers stood still and stared in disbelief. There, in front of them, was a U.S. soldier speaking to them in perfect Japanese. Guy "Gabby" Gabaldon told the Japanese soldiers that it was in their best interest to surrender. But how had Gabaldon, a Mexican American, learned to speak Japanese so well? And how did his knowledge of the language help him capture more than 1,500 Japanese soldiers during World War II?

Gabby Gabaldon grew up in Los Angeles. There, he had been raised by a Japanese American family who taught him Japanese. When the United States entered World War II in 1941, Gabaldon enlisted and was sent to the South Pacific.

With his military unit, Gabaldon made his way into the rain forest on the island of Saipan. There, the Japanese soldiers were hiding in caves. They had been ordered to fight to the death. Risking his own life, Gabaldon approached the front of the caves where the Japanese soldiers were dug in. Gabaldon used his language abilities to coax them out. He promised them good treatment if they surrendered.

Gabaldon's peaceful capture of these soldiers prevented a bloody battle and saved many lives. It also allowed U.S. forces to gain a great deal of information from the captured soldiers. This information saved additional lives as the Americans took control of the island.

For his bravery, Gabaldon received the Silver Star medal. In 1960, he was given the Navy Cross, the second highest naval award for bravery in battle.

1 Serving in Early Wars

Gabby Gabaldon is just one of many Mexican Americans who have served their country in times of war and crisis. Mexican Americans and other Latinos have aided or served in the U.S. armed forces since the birth of the nation.

The American Revolution and Spain

During the American Revolution (1775–1783), Spain controlled the Louisiana Territory. This vast region stretched east to the Mississippi River and west to the Rocky Mountains.

The Louisiana Territory lay west of the 13 British colonies. Spain saw Britain as its chief rival in North America. It was eager to weaken Britain's hold on its colonies.

After the American colonists declared their independence, they asked the Spanish for aid. The **Patriots,** as American colonists who fought for independence were called, asked for guns, gunpowder, blankets, medicine, and other supplies. Bernardo de Gálvez, the Spanish governor of Louisiana, agreed to help. Gálvez set up a supply line for the Patriots. Gálvez also convinced the king of Spain to secretly lend the Patriots large sums of money.

Spain's support of the Patriots had to be kept a secret. Officially, Spain was neutral. That meant it supported neither side in the war. However, that changed in 1779. Fearing a British invasion of Louisiana, Spain declared war on Britain. Gálvez now led his forces against the British along the Mississippi River and in Florida. This attack weakened the British army by forcing it to divide its resources between two enemies: the Patriots and Spain.

Many historians doubt that the Patriots could have won the war without the help Spain and Gálvez provided. Since there was not yet a country named Mexico in the 1770s, Bernardo de Gálvez is not considered to be Mexican American. However, most of Gálvez's funds, supplies, and soldiers came from the land that would become Mexico in 1821.

Mexican Americans and the Civil War

After the American Revolution, the United States began to expand westward. First, it purchased the Louisiana Territory in 1803. In 1819, it seized

Florida from Spain. Then, in 1845, the United States admitted Texas as a state. With the defeat of Mexico in the Mexican American War (1846–1848), the United States took about half of Mexico's land. The U.S. borders stretched from the Atlantic in the east to the Pacific in the west.

During the 1840s and 1850s, the United States was torn by disputes over slavery. The most critical issue was whether slavery would be permitted in the new western territories. The South pushed hard for the expansion of slavery to the west. The North strongly opposed it. A number of **compromises** were attempted. A compromise is a settlement of a dispute in which each side gives in a little. None of the compromises held. In the end, the question of slavery led to the bloodiest war ever fought on American soil: the Civil War (1860–1865).

Mexican Americans played important parts in that war. Some fought for the South, or the Confederacy. Others fought for the North, or the Union. Which side Mexican Americans fought for depended mainly on where they lived. California was a free state, or a state that did not permit slavery within its borders. Most Mexican Americans who lived there supported the Union. Captain Salvador Vallejo of California, for example, led a unit of 450 Mexican American cavalry for the Union. These troops helped stop Confederates from taking over New Mexico.

Lieutenant Colonel Manuel Cháves joined the New Mexico volunteers and fought for the Union. Captain Roman Anthony Baca, also a member of the New Mexico volunteers, served as a Union spy in Texas. However, there were also four units of Mexican American volunteers in New Mexico that chose to fight for the Confederacy.

In Texas, a slave state, Mexican Americans tended to join the Confederate army. One Texas unit was commanded by Colonel Santos Benavides, of Laredo. Benavides was the highest-ranking Mexican American in the Confederate army. In March 1864, he led his forces against the Union army in Brownsville. Outnumbered by Union troops, Benavides managed to drive the Union army away.

Active Learning: Who from this section would you like to interview if you were given the chance? Write down the questions you would ask.

The Civil War pitted the North against the South. While some Mexican Americans fought for the Union in the North, others fought for the Confederacy in the South.

2 The World at War

Two horrible world wars occurred in the 20th century. The United States fought in both of those wars, and Mexican Americans contributed to the war effort each time.

World War I: "The Great War"

World War I pitted Germany and its allies against Britain, France, Russia, and their allies. The war in Europe began in 1914, but the United States did not enter the war until 1917. When it did enter, it joined on the side of Britain and France.

There were a number of reasons why Mexican Americans might not have strongly supported the war effort. At the beginning of the 20th century, Mexican Americans faced widespread discrimination from Anglos. Many Anglos considered Mexican Americans to be foreigners. To make matters worse, Germany had sent a secret message to Mexico called the Zimmermann telegram. In the telegram, Germany offered to return Texas, New Mexico, and Arizona to Mexico if Mexico joined Germany against the United States. Mexico refused to join the war. But when the Zimmermann telegram became public in the United States, many Anglos accused Mexicans and Mexican Americans of sympathizing with Germany.

Despite the prejudice they faced, Mexican Americans contributed bravely to the war effort. David Barkley was one of these brave soldiers. Barkley was the first Mexican American to win the Medal of Honor. Sadly, he won the medal after his death. In 1918, Barkley gave his life in battle in France.

Barkley and a fellow soldier volunteered to swim the icy and dangerous Meuse (m'yuze) River to gather information about German positions. After crossing the river, they crept behind enemy lines and drew maps. As they were making their way back, they were discovered. The Germans began to shoot at them. The two U.S. soldiers made it back to the river and began to swim across. Barkley drowned, but the other soldier made it across safely.

For years, no one realized that Barkley was Mexican American. In the army, he had kept his heritage a secret to avoid discrimination. It was not until 1989 that his true heritage became publicly known. In September 1989, a special ceremony was held to honor this man, who had given his life for his country.

On the Home Front

Back in the United States, Mexican Americans served the war effort in a number of important ways. Like other Americans, they planted and harvested cotton and other crops that provided supplies and food for the troops.

The war also created an industrial boom in midwestern cities of the United States. Many Mexican Americans migrated, or moved, to these cities. They worked in coal mines, steel plants, meat packing houses, automobile plants, and in other industries. By the end of World War I, Mexican American communities had sprung up all over the Midwest.

The Veterans Return Home

With the end of World War I in 1918, Mexican American veterans began to return home.

Having just risked their lives to serve their country, they expected to be honored and respected. Of course, the Mexican American community welcomed them home. But to their disappointment, the returning veterans found that discrimination in the United States was as widespread as ever.

However, the war had strengthened the resolve of many Mexican Americans to fight harder against discrimination. One World War I veteran, Luz Sáenz, founded the Order of Sons of America (OSA) in 1921. OSA was a group that fought to win for Mexican Americans and other Latinos "all the rights and privileges . . . extended by the American Constitution."

World War II

In the years immediately following World War I, the U.S. economy was thriving, and most people had jobs. Then in the 1930s, the economy plunged into a depression. Although the Great Depression affected nearly every American, Mexican Americans and members of other ethnic groups were among the first to lose their jobs and homes. They suffered even more discrimination as they competed with Anglos for work.

Once again, however, when their nation needed them, Mexican Americans stepped up to volunteer. More than 250,000 Mexican Americans enlisted in the armed forces in World War II.

Along with other U.S. soldiers, many Mexican Americans were shipped overseas to fight against Germany and its allies during World War I. A number of Mexican Americans, such as David Barkley, lost their lives serving their country.

Mexican Americans Enlist

During World War II, it was common for all the men of a Mexican American family to enlist in the army. Socorro Delgado from Tucson, Arizona, recalled:

> *When the Second World War started, my brother José, my brother-in-law, my cousins, and my cousins' husbands served. At one time there were as many as 15 of our immediate family who had gone to war!*

Thousands of Mexican Americans went off to fight in the South Pacific. At the start of this case study, you read about Gabby Gabaldon. His story is just one example of the bravery many Mexican American soldiers showed during battle.

Early in the war, the U.S. military stationed many Mexican Americans in the Philippine Islands. Some military historians estimate that Mexican Americans made up about 25 percent of the soldiers in the battle of Bataan (bah-TAHN) Peninsula in 1942.

Early in the war, the Japanese trapped a large force of Americans on the peninsula. Ralph Rodriguez was one of the 16,000 U.S. soldiers who were captured during the battle.

After the battle, the prisoners were taken on an 85-mile march to prison camps. About 6,000 of the 16,000 Americans soldiers died on Bataan "Death March." Rodriguez survived was taken to a prisoner-of-war camp. He was held at the camp under harsh conditions for 34 months. Many Americans died in the camp. Rodriguez and his fellow prisoners were fi freed by U.S. troops near the end of the w

Many Mexican Americans also serve in units in Europe. One unit that included a large number of Mexican Americans was nicknamed the "Blue Devils." Manny Mendoza was a sergeant in this unit. A reporter for *The Saturday Evening Post* told of Mendoza's heroism during a battle in Italy:

> *Word drifted down that this time the enemy might drive us off* [Mount Battaglia in Italy]. *Manny Mendoza, the "Arizona Kid"*

> *from Mesa . . . headed for the crest. Standing against the skyline, Manny fired every weapon he could lay his hands on and broke the attack. They found 40 dead in front of Manny's position.*

During World War II, Mexican Americans won 17 Medals of Honor. After the war General Jonathan Wainwright, who had commanded the U.S. forces during the Bataan battle, noted:

> *In combat, we asked no questions about a man's background so long as we knew him to be a soldier. The part played in World War II* [by Mexican American] *men and women . . . was considerable. Almost every unit in the United States Army included Mexican American soldiers and they served well.*

Help from the Home Front

Like other Americans, Mexican Americans made solid contributions on the home front during World War II.

Mexican Americans bought large amounts of war bonds to raise money for the war. They sent gift packages to Mexican Americans stationed overseas. Mexican American men and women also worked in factories and in the fields.

Mexican American women served in the armed forces and worked in defense industries. A number of Mexican American women were bilingual. They spoke two languages: Spanish and English. The armed forces encouraged these women to join the service as interpreters and **cryptographers**, or code-breakers.

Fighting Prejudice

World War II ended in 1945. Once again, Mexican American veterans came home to face discrimination and prejudice. In the Southwest, Mexican Americans were barred from some restaurants and stores. Their children were sometimes not allowed to attend Anglo schools. Discrimination kept some Mexican American

Many Mexican American women contributed to the war effort during World War II by working in industries that suffered from labor shortages. The women shown here were railroad workers during the war. Most were Mexican American. Other Mexican American women served as interpreters or code-breakers during the war.

soldiers from getting benefits to which they were entitled under the **GI Bill**. The GI Bill guaranteed veterans low-cost housing and four years of education, among other benefits.

Furious about these acts of discrimination, many Mexican Americans decided to fight back. One example of the Mexican American community fighting prejudice centers on Felix Longoria. Longoria, a Mexican American from Texas, died a heroic death during World War II.

However, when his body was returned home, the undertaker refused to bury him in the town's cemetery or hold services for him in the chapel. Even in death, Felix Longoria could not escape prejudice because of his heritage.

The situation came to the attention of another Mexican American World War II veteran, Dr. Hector García. García took up Longoria's cause and fought to get him the hero's burial he deserved. García contacted Lyndon Johnson, who was then a U.S. senator from Texas. Senator Johnson helped to arrange for Longoria's burial in Arlington National Cemetery. There, Longoria received full military honors.

The GI Forum

Hector García's work did not begin or end with the burial of Felix Longoria. García founded the GI Forum in 1948, approximately a year before the Longoria incident. Its mission was to fight discrimination against Mexican American and other Latino veterans.

In an interview, García explained why Latinos needed an organization like the GI Forum:

> *The Forties world was very different. We had discrimination everywhere. We had no opportunities. We had to pay to vote. We had segregated schools. We were not allowed to go into public places. We were not allowed to buy land either, except in the barrios [Mexican American neighborhoods].*

The GI Forum grew from a local organization into a national organization. It has continued until this day to help Latino veterans gain full civil rights and benefits.

Thinking It Over

1. In general, how were Mexican American veterans treated upon their return from war?
2. **Comparing** Read the quotes by General Wainwright on page 59 and Dr. Hector García on this page. How would you compare the treatment of Mexican American soldiers during the war with the treatment they received back home?

Active Learning: If you were to interview one of the people mentioned in this section, what would you ask? Add your questions to the sheet you began in Section 1.

3 Modern-Day War Heroes

After World War II, the United States was directly involved in three other major conflicts: the Korean War, the Vietnam War, and the Persian Gulf War. Mexican Americans served bravely in each of these wars.

The Korean War

The United States fought the Korean War from 1950 to 1953. One of the many Mexican Americans to serve in the Korean War was Eugene Obregon of Los Angeles. Obregon sacrificed his own life to save the life of a fellow soldier. For his heroism, he was awarded the Medal of Honor. Obregon's brave deed is remembered in a monument in Los Angeles. Although Obregon is the focus of the monument, it has been built to honor all Latino winners of the Medal of Honor.

Mexican American women also participated in the Korean conflict. Jeanne E. Rivera was a U.S. Army nurse who cared for the wounded during the war. Rivera also served in the Vietnam War. There she earned a Bronze Star for giving aid to U.S. soldiers while she was under fire.

The War in Vietnam

The Vietnam War was a long and frustrating war for the United States. As the war went on,

Vietnam War veteran Master Sergeant Roy Benavidez (right) stands with actor James Edward Olmos. Benavidez won a Medal of Honor for bravery.

backgrounds. Often they were treated like outcasts. It took years for the nation to come to terms with the Vietnam War. When it did, it honored some of its heroes in a special way. One veteran who received a special tribute was Alfredo "Freddie" Gonzalez, a Mexican American Marine Corps sergeant. Gonzalez had died in combat in Vietnam in 1968.

On a cold day in February 1995, Gonzalez's mother Dolia smashed a bottle of champagne into the hull of a Navy destroyer. Then, choking back tears, she said, "I christen thee, Gonzalez." That moment was a special one for Mrs. Gonzalez and her friends and relatives. They had traveled from Edinburg, Texas, to the coast of Maine to christen the ship that honors Freddie Gonzalez.

Just 21 years old, Freddie Gonzalez perished during the first month of the Tet Offensive. The Tet Offensive was a major campaign by the communist Vietcong to drive the United States from Vietnam.

Everett Alvarez, Jr., was more fortunate than Freddie Gonzalez. Alvarez, a commander in the U.S. Navy, returned home from Vietnam alive. But Alvarez endured the longest captivity of any American during the Vietnam War. His

it became more unpopular in the United States. During the late 1960s and early 1970s, Mexican Americans were among the many groups protesting the war. In August 1970, members of a Mexican American group called the Brown Berets staged a huge demonstration against the war. The group protested the high number of Mexican Americans being drafted into the war.

The percentage of Mexican Americans who were killed in Vietnam was extremely high. For example, for the state of Texas alone, Mexican Americans accounted for over 25 percent of all Americans killed in Vietnam.

The unpopularity of the war made life very difficult for returning soldiers of all ethnic

A Good Book to Read

The Three Wars of Roy Benavidez, by Roy P. Benavidez and Oscar Griffin. Corona Books, San Antonio, 1986.

In this gripping book, Vietnam veteran and Medal of Honor winner Roy Benavidez tells his story. As a Mexican American, Benavidez faced much discrimination. He overcame many obstacles and was chosen to be a member of the Green Berets, a highly respected special military force.

Skyhawk fighter plane was shot down over the Gulf of Tonkin in August 1964. Alvarez was held as a prisoner of war for more than eight years. For his service, he won the Silver Star, two Legions of Merit, two Bronze Stars, two Purple Hearts, and the Distinguished Flying Cross.

The Persian Gulf War

Because of the unpopularity of the Vietnam War, most Vietnam veterans did not receive the kind of homecoming they deserved. In contrast, veterans of the Persian Gulf War (1990–1991) received warm welcomes when they returned. The Persian Gulf War was a war waged by the United States and its allies against Iraq in the Middle East. It began when Iraq invaded the neighboring country of Kuwait.

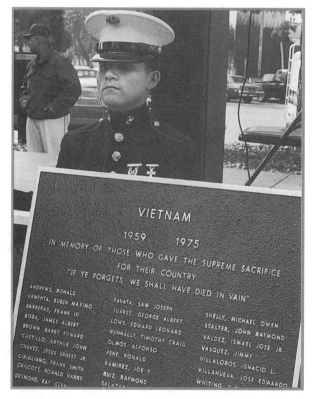

Many Mexican Americans fought and died in the Vietnam War. The memorial shown here honors several of those who lost their lives in the war.

Mexican American veterans of the Persian Gulf War were treated to an especially lively homecoming in Los Angeles. In April 1991, a parade on Olvera Street celebrated their return. Veteran Maria Lomeli-Conant told reporters, "It's really a good feeling for all of the people who are returning." She appreciated that the community was making the veterans feel really special.

During the parade, political leaders waved and shook hands. Family members and friends lined the street to honor veterans of the Persian Gulf War. The veterans enjoyed the celebration. Rodolfo Alvarez summed up the feelings of veterans of all wars when he said, "It's a tremendous feeling to be home."

A Tradition of Bravery and Courage

As you have read, Mexican Americans have participated in every major war in U.S. history. As an ethnic group, they have won more Medals of Honor than any other group.

Despite their contributions, they have often been subject to discrimination and prejudice. This situation, however, is changing as more Mexican Americans and other Latinos rise to positions of importance in government and the military. In addition, organizations such as the GI Forum have done a great deal to fight for the rights of Latinos.

Thinking It Over

1. How was Freddie Gonzalez honored for his contribution in the Vietnam War?
2. **Comparing** How was the treatment of returning veterans of the Vietnam War different from the treatment of returning veterans of the Persian Gulf War?

Going to the Source

Mexican Americans Go to War

The song below is called a folk ballad. This ballad was sung by young Mexican American recruits from Texas during World War I. The recruits were on their way to fight in France in 1918.

Register of 1918

Good bye Laredo, highlighted
by your towers and bells,
but we shall never forget
your beautiful Mexican women.

They are taking us to fight
to some distant land
and taking us to fight
the German troops.

They are taking us to fight
in separate directions
and taking us to fight
with different nations.

Registro de 1918

Adiós Laredo lucido
con sus torres y campanas,
pero nunca olvidaremos
a tus lindas mexicanas.

Ya nos llevan a pelear
a unas tierras muy lejanas
y nos llevan a pelear
con las tropas alemanas.

Ya nos llevan a pelear
en separadas direcciones,
y nos llevan a pelear
con diferentes naciones.

1. Where are the soldiers being taken to fight?
2. Who is the enemy that the soldiers are going to fight?
3. **Analyzing a Song** What feelings does the song express? Explain.

Case Study Review

Identifying Main Ideas

1. What motivated Bernardo de Gálvez and Spain to help the Patriots during the American Revolution?

2. How did Mexican Americans on the home front contribute to the World War II effort?

3. Why did Dr. Hector García found the GI Forum?

Working Together

Work with two or three other students to design a monument in honor of Mexican American soldiers. Sketch a design for your monument and write a paragraph for a plaque to go on the monument. Then write a speech to give at the dedication of your group's monument. Present your design, plaque, and speech to your class.

Active Learning

Interviewing Choose a partner to work with. Together, review the notes you took while reading this case study. Decide which person from the case study you wish to interview. Write seven to ten questions to ask that person during the interview. Also, be sure to write the answers to the questions. Then use the questions and answers to role play the interview. One of you will be the interviewer, and the other will play the role of the war veteran who is being interviewed.

Lessons for Today

As you have read, Mexican American veterans have often returned from wars only to face discrimination and prejudice. You have read that World War I soldier David Barkley decided to keep his Mexican heritage a secret. Do you think Mexican Americans would be likely to do this today? Why or why not?

What Would You Have Done?

During the American Revolution, Mexico was a Spanish colony. Imagine that you lived in Spanish Mexico during the American Revolution. Would you have supported the Patriots' fight against the British? Why or why not?

CRITICAL THINKING

Supporting Generalizations

The Language of Thinking

Generalizations

The following is a list of words that may signal a generalization.

- almost
- usually
- most
- many
- often
- some
- perhaps
- seldom

A generalization is a broad statement that is meant to apply to many cases. Generalizations are useful because they allow speakers or writers to sum up a broad idea in a brief statement. It is important, however, to support, or back up, generalizations with facts. If a generalization cannot be backed up with facts, it may be inaccurate.

Below are generalizations about Mexican American participation in the U.S. armed forces. Copy each generalization into your notebook. Then review the case study and write down two to three facts to back up each generalization. As an example, the first generalization has been completed.

1. Since the birth of the nation, many Mexican Americans have defended the United States bravely and with distinction.

   Facts:
   - Mexican Americans have won more Medals of Honor than any other ethnic group.
   - The stories of people like Santos Benavides, David Barkley, and Freddie Gonzalez stand as proof of the bravery with which Mexican Americans fought.

2. During the Civil War, both the Union and the Confederate armies included Mexican American soldiers.

3. Despite having served in their nation's armed forces, many Mexican Americans suffered discrimination.

4. Many Mexican American women served in the U.S. armed forces during a number of conflicts.

Dolores Huerta has been fighting for the rights of migrant farm workers since the 1960s. Here, she addresses a crowd at a 1972 rally.

DOLORES HUERTA: WORKING FOR JUSTICE

CRITICAL QUESTIONS

- Under what conditions did migrant farm workers live during the 1940s and 1950s?
- How did Dolores Huerta and the United Farm Workers help to improve the lives of migrant farm workers?

TERMS TO KNOW

- migrant workers
- labor union
- Chicano
- strike
- boycott
- lobby

ACTIVE LEARNING

How would it feel to be friends with Dolores Huerta? As you read this case study, imagine that you are her friend. In this exercise, you will write diary entries about important events in Huerta's life. Your diary entries should describe your feelings about these events. Look for the Active Learning hint boxes located throughout the case study. They will help you create the entries.

They came from all parts of California. They were young and old, farm workers and factory workers, teachers and students. There were mothers pushing children in strollers and people pushing themselves in wheelchairs.

They marched along the two-lane state highway in a long, thin line. As they marched, they waved banners and shouted slogans. Around them, barley fields and orange groves stretched as far as the eye could see. The year was 1994.

"¡Viva La Causa!" they shouted. "Long live 'the cause!'"

Leading the group was a tiny, gray-haired woman, who was less than five feet tall. A 64-year-old grandmother, she was as full of energy as the youngest marchers. Her name was Dolores Huerta.

Twenty-eight years earlier, Huerta had traveled this same route. At that time, she had helped lead farm workers on a march from the town of Delano to the state capital of Sacramento. In 1966, as they passed from town to town, the marchers faced the hostility of farm owners. In 1994, they were invited to lunch at the local chambers of commerce.

The 1966 march helped make Americans aware of the plight of the nation's migrant farm workers. The 1994 march reminded the nation that more progress was needed.

"We are on the second wave of history," said Dolores Huerta to the marchers. "Walk the streets with us into history."

1 Finding Her Calling

Dolores Huerta described the mission that she has spent a lifetime serving in three simple words: "Work for justice." For more than 40 years, Huerta has worked for justice for thousands of migrant farm workers.

With her friend César Chávez, Dolores Huerta formed a union of farm workers in the 1960s. Many of their friends thought it was impossible to establish a successful farm workers union. Before Huerta and Chávez came along, there had been many attempts to form a farm workers union. All had ended in failure. The reasons for the failures were clear. Each day, exhausted farm workers came home from the fields after hours of hard work. Few had the time and energy to fight for higher wages, better housing, and safer working conditions.

The task facing Huerta was even more difficult because she was Mexican American *and* a woman. Mexican Americans faced a lifetime of prejudice. As a woman, a wife, and a mother, Huerta faced an additional burden. In the 1960s, most people in the United States believed that mothers should stay at home. Despite these obstacles, Huerta decided to lead the fight to win rights for migrant farm workers.

Desperate Conditions

When Huerta began her mission, migrant farm workers lived a harsh life. They worked in the hot sun for hours, picking crops such as grapes, tomatoes, and cotton. Some owners made workers pay for the water they drank on the job during the day. Often there were no toilets in the fields. After 14 to 16 hours of grueling labor, workers might return home with as little as five dollars. From this salary, they had to buy food and pay rent for the run-down shacks or cheap motel rooms in which they lived. Though they harvested food all day, farm workers and their families often went hungry.

Farm workers also had to move constantly from one state to another to harvest different crops. They were known as **migrant workers** because they migrated, or moved, from one area to another. When migrant workers were finished harvesting a crop in one place, they no longer had a job. They had to move to a different area where the crops were ready to be harvested.

This was hard on the workers, but it was even harder on their children. They had to keep changing schools in the middle of the year. Few children went to the same school for any length of time. As a result, few finished school. For example, César Chávez left school in the eighth grade. By that time, he had attended more than 30 different schools in California.

From New Mexico to California

Dolores Huerta was born in 1930 in the mining town of Dawson, New Mexico. Her father, Juan Fernandez, was a coal miner. Unhappy with working conditions, Mr. Fernandez became a union organizer. A union organizer is someone who signs up workers to join a **labor union**, an organization that fights for better conditions for workers.

Huerta grew up during the Great Depression, a period during which the U.S. economy was in decline. The Depression took place during the 1930s. It was a time when there were not enough jobs for Americans. People bought less food and other goods. Factories closed, and wages fell. With factories producing fewer goods, there was less demand for coal. So it was hard to find work in the mines.

To make a living, Mr. Fernandez became a migrant worker. He labored in fields in Colorado, Nebraska, and Wyoming. His dedication to the labor union and his life as a migrant worker made a lasting impression on young Huerta.

The Depression was a hard time for most Americans, but it was especially difficult for migrant worker families. Since people were buying less food, there was less need for workers to harvest crops. Most farm workers worked fewer days and for lower wages than in previous years.

When Huerta was six, her parents divorced. Her father stayed in New Mexico, returned to school, and received a college degree. In 1938, he won election to the New Mexico state legislature. He worked hard for laws protecting workers. Huerta was proud of her father's accomplishments.

After the divorce, Huerta, her mother, and her two brothers settled in Stockton, California. Huerta's mother worked as a waitress at night and in a food processing plant during the day. Later she opened a boarding house. A boarding house provides rooms and food for guests. Huerta and her brothers did much of the work at the boarding house. Often Huerta's mother gave rooms to farm worker families for free.

Huerta's mother believed strongly in educating her children in their culture and the arts. She encouraged them to play musical instruments and to attend concerts. As a teenager, Huerta studied tap dancing, ballet, and regional Mexican dances. She dreamed of becoming a professional dancer.

Facing Prejudice

As a child, Huerta did not see much prejudice. She lived in a neighborhood with great ethnic variety. Huerta recalls, "I was raised in Stockton in an integrated neighborhood. There were Chinese, Latinos, Native Americans, Blacks, Japanese, Italians, and others."

When she entered high school, things changed. Huerta received straight A's for the compositions she had written for her high school English class. However, her teacher refused to give her an A for the course. "I asked the teacher why," recalled Huerta. "She said that she thought my work was too good and that someone had to be writing the papers for me!" The teacher did not believe that a Mexican American could write so well. The experience had a lasting effect on Huerta. It made her aware of how Mexican Americans were often treated.

After high school, Huerta married, had two children, and worked as a clerk. Then she decided to pursue a career in teaching. She took night courses at Stockton College. Huerta was the only Mexican American in the school. At first, she felt out of place there. Then her mother took her on a trip to Mexico City. This experience made her proud of her own rich heritage as a Mexican American.

Inspired by her trip, she joined different **Chicano** organizations. *Chicano* is a term used by some Mexican Americans to express pride in their heritage. She also decided to do something that would really make a difference.

Huerta had gone into teaching in order to help others. But her teaching job did not last long. She felt frustrated. "I couldn't do anything for the kids who came to school barefoot and hungry," she later said. "I thought I could do more by organizing farm workers than by trying to teach their hungry children."

Active Learning: Imagine that you are Dolores Huerta's friend. For your first diary entry, think about the discussion Huerta had with her teacher about her English grade. Write a diary entry that recounts what Huerta told you and how you feel about it.

Getting Involved

Soon after she left teaching, Huerta got the chance to help the farm workers and their families. She joined an organization called the Community Service Organization (CSO), a civil rights group. The main goal of the CSO was to register, or sign up, Mexican Americans to vote.

Huerta joined the effort to get people to register. This was tough work. Many poor Mexican Americans moved from place to place. With no permanent residence, they could not register to vote. Many could not read or write. Others could not prove they were U.S. citizens. But Huerta succeeded in getting thousands of people registered. She possessed a knack for persuading others and gaining their trust.

As part of her job, Huerta visited the homes of the farm workers. She was deeply disturbed by the living conditions she saw. Many farm worker families were living in very harsh conditions.

"We would see their dirty floors, the wooden boxes for furniture," Huerta said. "They had no money for food and worked so hard."

Meeting César Chávez

While working at the CSO, Huerta met a young man named César Chávez. This man would eventually become the most important leader in the fight for the rights of migrant farm workers. Although he appeared shy, Chávez quickly showed his leadership skills and inspired other CSO members to continue their difficult work.

Chávez and his family had been migrant farm workers. He experienced the discrimination that Mexican Americans suffered and the terrible living conditions that all migrant workers endured.

The work that Chávez did at the CSO in the 1950s gave him the experience he later needed to organize farm workers. At first, he hated speaking in public. With practice, however, he became a powerful speaker. "The business of convincing a man is the business of spending time with him," Chávez explained. "You have to draw a picture and make it plain. You have to talk facts about things he can see. Theories don't work."

Huerta was impressed with Chávez's commitment to the CSO and wanted to work with him. Like Chávez, Huerta trained herself to become an effective public speaker. Chávez and Huerta soon were a team. This marked the beginning of a lifelong partnership between the two leaders.

In early 1962, Chávez brought up the topic of organizing farm workers. Huerta later described her reaction.

> *César said there will never be a union unless we organize it. I thought he was joking. People thought we were crazy. They asked, "How are you going to organize farm workers? They are poor, powerless immigrants. They don't have any money and they can't vote."*

However, Huerta soon realized that forming a union was critical to improving the lives of farm workers. Later that year, Huerta

Inspired by César Chavez's dedication, Huerta joined the effort to organize a union of migrant farm workers. Here, she registers representatives to a national meeting of farm workers in 1962. In time, the farm workers union would become Huerta's life work.

and Chávez formed the organization that grew into the United Farm Workers (UFW).

Thinking It Over

1. Give two reasons why it was difficult to organize migrant farm workers.
2. **Analyzing** How did experiences in her youth prepare Huerta for her role as a union organizer?

2 The UFW Goes to Work

In 1962, Huerta and Chávez began to sign up farm workers in the Central Valley of California to join the union. In order to do this, the two leaders had to leave their families at home and drive from town to town. It was hard work, but it paid off. By 1965, they had signed up about 1,200 workers. Most of them were Mexican American migrant workers, but others were Filipino and African American.

The movement also gained the support of a number of religious organizations. One of them was the California Migrant Ministry, a group of clergy that had pledged to help farm workers. The California bishops of the Catholic Church also backed the farm workers in their struggles.

In 1965, the UFW joined a **strike**, or walkout, against grape producers. The strike was started by the Agricultural Workers Organizing Committee (AWOC), a mostly Filipino union headed by Larry Itlong. After supporting AWOC, the UFW decided to widen the strike. It struck against table grape growers in California's San Joaquin Valley. The strike called attention to poor working conditions and low wages. Farm workers were earning $1.25 an hour and 10 cents for every box of grapes they picked. The union demanded $1.40 an hour and 25 cents per box.

This was the start of *La Causa*, or the Cause. This was the name the farm workers gave to their movement. La Causa was about more than wages. It expressed the dignity and pride of Mexican Americans and their determination to preserve their culture.

"Totally Fearless"

The grape growers fought the strikers by spraying them with pesticides, which are poisons used to kill insects. The growers also shut off the strikers' electricity and piled their belongings on the road.

Huerta faced the strike as she had faced other challenges in her life. She set to work with complete courage and energy. "Dolores was totally fearless, both mentally and physically,"

Dolores Huerta talks to grape pickers early in the grape strike. She explains to them the value of joining the union and the strike. Later, the union would intensify the effect of the strike by staging a boycott on grapes.

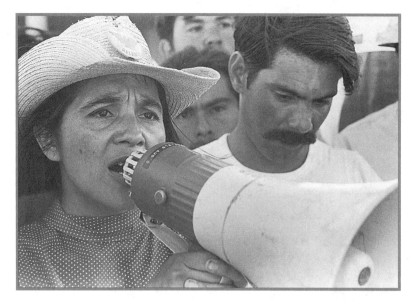

Dolores Huerta worked tirelessly to organize the farm workers union. She spread the message that workers could gain power through the union.

Chávez said. He recalled that when things became difficult during the first strike, some of the strikers talked of giving up the struggle and going back to work the next morning. Dolores would not hear of this. Before dawn, Huerta and Chávez drove around to workers' homes to see if any of them were getting ready to go to work. When they found workers who wanted to go to work, they would jump out of their truck and convince them not to break the strike.

Active Learning: Write a diary entry describing Dolores Huerta's commitment to La Causa. What sacrifices did she make for the cause? What qualities does she have that you admire as her friend?

The March

As the strike continued, Huerta and Chávez searched for a way to publicize their cause. They found it in a march.

For 25 days, Chávez and Huerta and 67 other farm workers marched through central California. They started in the farming town of Delano and ended in the state capital of Sacramento. Over the 330-mile trip, they walked in single file behind the black eagle banner of the union. Some marchers carried signs bearing the single Spanish word *¡Huelga!*, or strike.

Local police tried to keep them out of towns along the way. But the farm workers would not be turned back. As they marched, their numbers grew. By the time they reached Sacramento, they numbered more than 10,000. Many marchers arrived in Sacramento with their feet badly swollen and blistered. On the steps of the state capitol building, they held a massive rally that was reported throughout the nation.

The Boycott

In January 1968, Huerta and 60 union members set out in an old bus for a 3,000-mile trip to New York City. New York City was the largest single market for California grapes. The purpose of the trip was to organize a **boycott**. A boycott is a refusal to buy a product until certain demands are met. The union members wanted to convince consumers and store owners not to buy California grapes. Huerta and the others distributed information and spoke to community organizations.

Some of the farm workers got out along the way to arrange boycotts in other cities. Eventually, more than 200 workers organized boycotts in 400 communities across the United States. Publicizing the boycott was tougher than the workers expected. Huerta recalled:

When we got to New York, it was something like four or five degrees above zero. The first day we went out on the picket line, one of the Filipino women fell down and hit her head on some ice and had amnesia [loss of memory] for about an hour. Everybody was slipping on the ice and falling. But they had a heck of a lot of spirit.

For several years, Huerta led the boycott efforts. The union's efforts cut badly into the sale of California grapes. The boycott ended in 1970, when growers agreed to a contract that would raise wages and improve conditions in the fields. It was the first big labor victory for migrant workers in the United States!

With the strike over, Huerta took a leading role in negotiating other contracts between the union and other growers. She was elected vice president of the UFW in 1972. She then headed the 1975 grape, lettuce, and wine boycotts. These boycotts helped pass the first California law that guaranteed farm workers secret-ballot union elections. Secret ballots meant that the workers' votes were private. That way, owners would have no way of knowing who voted for the union and who did not. In the following months, UFW candidates won almost half of the 406 local elections.

Thinking It Over

1. What is a boycott?
2. **Expressing Opinions** Would you boycott a company that treated its workers unfairly? Why or why not?

3 Serving La Causa

By 1972, the California-based union had more than 100,000 members and had joined the AFL-CIO, the country's most powerful union. It had also inspired farm workers to organize unions in Texas, Arizona, and several midwestern states. As vice president of the UFW, Huerta spent an increasing amount of time lobbying. To **lobby** means to seek to influence public officials to pass new laws. Huerta's lobbying efforts took her to lawmakers in Sacramento and Washington, D.C. Huerta also organized strikes, directed UFW boycotts, and led farm worker campaigns for political candidates.

In strikes during the 1970s and 1980s, Huerta often faced hostile actions by the growers. She was also arrested 22 times, mostly for violating anti-strike court orders. In spite of these obstacles, Huerta continued to fight for La Causa.

For this effort, Huerta has won the respect of many political leaders and citizens around the country. Eleanor Smeal, president of The Feminist Majority Foundation, described Huerta as a "dedicated, inspired leader." Said Smeal, "She is the hardest working, most determined, yet optimistic crusader for people I have met."

Lobbying for Change

Huerta spoke out often against pesticides. Doctors had found high rates of cancer and birth defects among migrant workers. Many people believe that the pesticides sprayed on crops caused these conditions. Huerta argued that these chemicals threatened farm workers and consumers alike. Under her leadership, the union began to fight the use of pesticides in the fields. Because of the union's efforts, many of the more dangerous pesticides were banned.

Huerta also successfully worked for state laws that removed citizenship requirements for public assistance. Her success meant that migrant workers and others who were not U.S. citizens could now apply for help from the government. She got the state assembly to pass laws that created insurance programs for farm workers.

Although Huerta was a tough negotiator, she hated violence. She was largely responsible for the union's policy of non-violence. Many years later, she said that this was one of her proudest accomplishments.

I think we brought to the world . . . the whole idea of boycotting as a non-violent tactic. I think we showed the world that non-violence can work to make social change.

Overcoming Obstacles

While working for labor justice, Huerta also raised a family of 11 children. Along the way, there were some rough periods with money, which was in short supply. The family once ate donated food and drank powdered milk for more than two years. Fresh milk was just too expensive.

As her children were growing up, Huerta was often away from home organizing workers. Sometimes, her younger children traveled with her. The older children often stayed with relatives or other union families.

All of the children coped with frequent moves. One of her sons, Emilio Huerta, is now an attorney for the union. He said:

As a labor organizer, my mother had to follow workers in their seasonal patterns, and we traveled around with her. Sometimes, we attended as many as three or four different schools in a year.

"At certain times, it was hard having a mom who always worked and wasn't your typical mother," said Maria Elena Chávez, one of Huerta's daughters who also works with the union. "As I get older, it becomes easier to understand why those sacrifices were made."

She added, "We have always known that we can overcome any obstacles with a lot of determination, time, and sacrifice."

A Good Movie to See

Chicano! History of the Mexican American Civil Rights Movement. Episode 2: "The Struggle in the Fields." Produced by the National Latino Communications Center and Galán Productions, Inc., in association with KCET/Los Angeles, 1996.

When the members of the UFW took to the streets to boycott, strike, and march, they risked their personal safety as well as the welfare of their families. This documentary brings that struggle to life. Watch this video, and you will witness Dolores Huerta, César Chávez, and others fight for the rights of migrant farm workers.

An Inspiration

The work of Huerta, Chávez, and others who founded the UFW inspired other Chicano leaders during the 1960s and 1970s. One such leader was Luis Valdez, today a famous playwright and film producer. Valdez was a recent college graduate when he began El Teatro Campesino, The Workers Theater, in 1965. The theater group entertained migrant farm workers and educated them about the strikes, the boycotts, and other issues.

Other leaders of the Chicano movement included José Angel Gutiérrez and Corky Gonzalez. Gutiérrez, from Crystal City, Texas, founded La Raza Unida, a Chicano political party. One goal of La Raza Unida was to serve as a unifying force in the Mexican American struggle for equality and identity.

In 1969, Corky Gonzalez organized the first Chicano Youth Liberation Conference in Denver, Colorado. The conference brought together

Dolores Huerta inspired migrant workers to join the union and fight for common goals. In 1979, these workers staged a strike to gain better working conditions in the fields.

representatives of Chicano youth groups. These leaders and others made the public aware of the injustices suffered by all Mexican Americans.

New Challenges

For many years, Huerta was concerned about who would guide the union when the older leaders were gone. By the late 1970s, many of the people running the organization had come from outside the movement. They were lawyers, accountants, and office managers, not farm workers.

Huerta believed that it was important to train the union's farm workers to run the UFW. She wanted the farm workers to have control over the actions and decisions that would affect their own lives. Under her direction, the UFW began to train farm workers in union business. This training included teaching English to Spanish-speaking farm workers. Huerta realized the importance of speaking English in order to communicate with growers, politicians, and the public.

Blazing New Trails

Dolores Huerta was the first woman in the UFW to occupy a high position within the organization. But she is not alone. Many of the services provided by the union are run by women.

For instance, the UFW has a credit union, which farm workers use as a bank. The UFW also runs clinics for its members. Workers can go to these clinics for medical help and health advice. Both the credit union and the clinics are run by women.

Still on the Move

Huerta's role in the history of the modern-day labor movement is unchallenged. Said Karen Nussbaum, director of the Women's Bureau of the U.S. Labor Department:

> *She is the most important woman labor leader of our time. She led the picket lines, stared down the bosses, negotiated the contracts, took the beatings, and carried on.*

Dolores Huerta did not shrink from danger. In 1988, she was in San Francisco to hand out brochures promoting the UFW's grape boycott. As police tried to move the protesters, Huerta fell to the ground in a crush of people. Rushed to the hospital, she had to have emergency surgery to save her life.

Approaching her 70th birthday, Huerta continued to work hard for her cause. She averaged less than four hours of sleep a night. She still spent much of her time traveling, organizing migrant workers, negotiating contracts with growers, and giving speeches.

For this effort, she received no salary from the union. The union paid for her rent, food, and medical expenses. She had not bought a new car for years. She still drove her same old car around central California, stopping to talk to workers in the fields. "We believe that you cannot help farm workers if you are so much richer than they are," she said.

Huerta kept a deep faith in Americans. "People in our country are fair. They want to see justice done," Huerta said. "I don't care what problems we have in this country. They can be solved by people working together."

For years, Chávez and Huerta worked together to build the UFW. Chávez died in 1993. Today, Huerta continues the work as vice president of the organization.

Thinking It Over

1. Why did Huerta believe it was important for farm workers to take over the leadership of the UFW?
2. **Drawing Conclusions** In what ways do you think Huerta serves as a role model to young people in the United States?

GOING TO THE SOURCE

The Elements of San Joaquin

Gary Soto is a Mexican American writer who often writes about the hardships of migrant laborers. After reading his poems, you may better understand what Dolores Huerta was fighting for.

Field

The wind sprays pale dirt into my mouth
The small, almost invisible scars
On my hands.

The pores in my throat and elbows
Have taken in a seed of dirt of their own.
After a day in the grape fields near Rolinda
A fine silt, washed by sweat,
Has settled into the lines
On my wrists and palms.

Already I am becoming the valley,
A soil that sprouts nothing
For any of us.

Field Poem

When the foreman whistled
My brother and I
Shouldered our hoes,
Leaving the field.
We returned to the bus
Speaking
In broken English, in broken Spanish.
The restaurant food,
The tickets to a dance
We wouldn't buy with our pay.

From the smashed bus window,
I saw the leaves of cotton plants
Like small hands
Waving good-bye.

From Gary Soto, *The Elements of San Joaquin*
Pittsburgh: University of Pittsburgh Press, 1977.

1. In "Field," why does Soto say that the soil sprouts nothing?
2. **Interpreting Poetry** What does the last stanza of "Field Poem" tell about the lives of migrant farm workers?

Case Study Review

Identifying Main Ideas

1. Why did Dolores Huerta give up teaching to organize a union?
2. How did the farm workers union first gain public attention?
3. How did the UFW improve working conditions for migrant farm workers?

Working Together

As you have read, Dolores Huerta used non-violent means to fight for her cause. Throughout history, many others have used non-violent means to achieve great things. Martin Luther King and Mohandas Gandhi are two others who have used non-violence. Form a small group and find out more about how either King or Gandhi used non-violent methods to achieve his goals. Present your findings to the class in an oral report.

Active Learning

Writing a Diary Entry Review and revise the two diary entries you wrote while reading the case study. Now write a final entry explaining what Dolores Huerta's life has meant to you.

Lessons for Today

"Our industry is very close to collapse. If we accept these terms, we will not be able to survive in the 21st century."

"The owners make millions of dollars. We have a right to decent conditions and the same freedoms as all Americans."

These arguments were given by California growers and farm workers during the labor strike of the 1960s. But these very same arguments were used by owners and players during the 1994-5 baseball strike. At the time, the owners were making hundreds of millions of dollars a year. The players had salaries that averaged about $1.5 million a year! Why did the millionaires of major league baseball use the same arguments as the people in the grape strike more than 30 years earlier? In what ways were the grape pickers' strike and the baseball strike similar and different?

What Might You Have Done?

Imagine that you are a farm worker who has been asked by the union to join the strike. Considering what the money you earn means to your family, would you strike or not? Explain your reasons in a brief paragraph.

Facts and Opinions

A fact is something that actually happened or is known to be true. A fact can be proved. Facts can be used to support points of view, or opinions. An opinion supported by many facts is often more reliable than an unsupported opinion.

People often have different **points of view**, or opinions, on important issues. Knowing how to interpret these points of view is part of being a good critical thinker. Below are two letters about the farm workers' struggle. Read these two letters and think about the arguments the writers make to support their points of view. Then answer the questions that follow.

March 27, 1965

I am fed up with news stories such as the one that appeared on March 15. Your story gives the impression that farm workers are unhappy. I can tell you that my workers are quite content with their conditions and wages.

The trouble is caused by outsiders who do not care about the welfare of the farm workers. They just want to destroy the industry. I will never give in to the unions.

William Sefton, grower

April 18, 1965

As one of those who marched from Delano to Sacramento, I was outraged by Mr. Sefton's letter. The truth is that we are striking not because of outsiders. We are striking for higher wages.

Sefton claims that workers are happy with their wages and conditions. I attended the meeting where the strike vote was taken. There was no doubt of the feelings of the workers. Nearly 2,000 voices called out ¡Huelga!, Strike!

Is it any wonder that we strike? Our members sweat in the fields for 16 hours a day and earn as little as five dollars. I know this because I grew up in a farm worker's family.

We do not want to destroy the farms. They are our livelihood. However, we will not stop our struggle until we are able to earn a decent wage and gain decent working conditions.

Helena Sanchez, worker

1. According to Sefton, who is responsible for the farm workers' strike?

2. Does Sanchez agree with this position? Why or why not?

3. Look back at both letters. Make a list of how many opinions in each is backed up by a fact. Then use your list to decide whose argument is more convincing.

The Brown Berets, along with other Chicano organizations, planned the August 1970 march in Los Angeles to protest the Vietnam War.

EL MOVIMIENTO: THE CHICANO MOVEMENT

CRITICAL QUESTIONS

- How and why did the Chicano Movement start?
- In what ways do the goals of the Chicano Movement continue today?

TERMS TO KNOW

- El Movimiento
- La Raza
- satire
- moratorium
- bilingual
- legacy

ACTIVE LEARNING

In this case study, you will read about the Chicano Movement. This movement involved Mexican Americans who were protesting for change. At the end of the case study, you will be asked to write a letter to the editor of a newspaper giving your opinion of the Chicano Movement. Take notes as you read and look for the hint boxes. They will help you to write the letter.

No one knew how the day would turn out. Over 30,000 Mexican Americans from all over the nation participated in a march in East Los Angeles on August 29, 1970. They marched peacefully, but they were also angry. They were angry that a large number of Mexican Americans were being sent to fight in the Vietnam War. They were also furious about the many incidents of police brutality against Mexican Americans. In that year alone, six innocent Mexican Americans in Los Angeles had been killed. All of these murders were believed to have been committed by the police.

The protesters marched for several miles to Laguna Park. There, they sat on the grass and listened to music while they waited for the program's speakers to begin.

Suddenly, they were being pushed by 500 police, who were outfitted with riot equipment. Without warning, the police began to fire tear gas at the men, women, and children. One of the women who marched recalled:

> Many of us collapsed from the gas, which not only blinded but also caused nausea.
> Hundreds of us took shelter in the homes of people living around the park . . . who were long aware of police brutality.

At the end of the day, three Mexican Americans had been killed by the police. This event turned the community's anger to rage. Buildings went up in flames that night in East Los Angeles. It seemed as if the Vietnam War had come home.

 A Time of Change

The East Los Angeles protest of August 1970 was not an unusual event during those times. In the 1960s and 1970s, many protests took place. Some remained peaceful, but others ended in violence. Many were staged by Native Americans, African Americans, and Mexican Americans calling for an end to discrimination and prejudice. Others were held by people of all ethnicities to protest to the Vietnam War.

Protesting for Justice

During the late 1950s and early 1960s, movements for change began forming across the United States. Among the earliest was the Civil Rights Movement begun by African Americans. Leaders of this movement used nonviolent tactics such as boycotts, sit ins, and picket lines to bring to the nation's attention the discrimination African Americans faced. In large part, the movement was run by young people.

As the 1960s wore on, the Vietnam War became a focus of protest. Many high school and university students organized and participated in anti-war protests. One concern of the protesters was U.S. involvement in another country's civil war. Another concern was that too many U.S. soldiers being drafted into the army were members of minority groups, such as African American or Mexican Americans.

Amid this atmosphere of protest, a number of groups began movements to fight for their civil and social rights. Native Americans, women, and Mexican Americans were among the groups to protest. They mainly focused on issues such as low wages and discrimination in education and employment.

Mexican Americans Fight for Change

The Mexican American struggle for justice is called **El Movimiento** or the Chicano Movement. During the 1960s, many Mexican Americans used the word *Chicano* to describe themselves. The term expressed pride in their Mexican heritage.

Another term used by Mexican Americans involved in El Movimiento was **La Raza.** Literally, the team *La Raza* means "the race." However, to those who used the term, it meant "the Mexican American people." Again, this term was used to express Mexican American pride.

Farm Workers Lead the Way

Before the start of the Chicano Movement, there was an earlier effort by migrant farm workers to form a union. For many years, migrant farm workers in California, Texas, and other states struggled in the fields to make a living. Migrant workers traveled from place to place to find seasonal work. They often labored under terrible conditions for low wages.

Guided by César Chávez, they began to protest for better wages and improved working conditions. Chávez was himself a migrant laborer.

Chávez and other Chicano leaders succeeded in organizing a union for migrant laborers. They called it the United Farm Workers (UFW). As the union won benefits for its members, Chávez gained national attention. Like Martin Luther King, Jr., the leader of the African American struggle for civil rights, Chávez believed in using nonviolence to gain rights. King's actions influenced Chávez. Chávez once said:

> I learned a lot from him [King] . . . And I was totally in awe with what he did . . . . I was an organizer, so I know what he was going through . . . so I got to know him and we became friends. And I began to see—I got involved with some of the things he was doing and then also looked to him for . . . advice, guidance.

Theater for the People

Chávez's hard work and dedication persuaded others to join the struggle for farm workers' rights. One young Chicano who became part of the movement was Luis Valdez, an aspiring young playwright. Valdez and his family had been migrant farm workers. Despite traveling from job to job, Valdez managed to finish high school and attend San Jose State College.

After meeting César Chávez in 1965, Valdez organized workers into El Teatro Campesino (The Worker's Theater). As he later recalled, there was "no money, no props, no scripts, no stage, no lights, no actors, nothing. All that there was was just the spirit of the people, but that was enough." Valdez's idea was to use theater performances to gain support for the strikes and boycotts of the UFW. El Teatro Campesino's

César Chávez led migrant farm workers in their effort to form the United Farm Workers (UFW) union. The UFW fought for better wages and working conditions for farm workers. Chávez's nonviolent approach won him many admirers. Here, he leads a strike, or huelga (HWEHL-gah).

During the moratorium of August 1970, thousands of Chicanos marched peacefully to Laguna Park to protest the Vietnam War and police brutality. There, they were attacked by police.

plays often used **satire,** or biting humor, to make their points. El Teatro Campesino used satire to ridicule the owners of the vineyards for whom the farm workers toiled.

Firm Goals, Peaceful Means

The work of Chávez and Valdez became the inspiration for a nonviolent Chicano Movement in the cities. Mexican Americans throughout the Southwest and Midwest fought discrimination and prejudice using nonviolent means.

When Chicanos organized a protest march, volunteers monitored the protesters' behavior. If a protester became violent, parade monitors would sternly warn him or her not to cause problems.

As El Movimiento progressed, its goals moved beyond higher wages and better working conditions. Tired of being shut out of good high schools, universities, and politics, Chicanos began to fight for their rights on larger issues. In the early 1970s, El Teatro Campesino worked to support the broader goals of El Movimiento. The goals of El Movimiento included respect for the Mexican American heritage, increased Chicano involvement in politics, and equal opportunities for Chicanos and all Latinos in business and education.

Active Learning: In your notes, write down what El Movimiento was. Also list some of its early leaders, the reasons they protested, and their goals. Use this information in your letter.

Thinking It Over

1. How did Luis Valdez use his talents to help the farm workers?
2. **Understanding Causes and Effects** How did the farm workers' movement affect the Chicano Movement?

2 The Movement Takes a New Direction

For the most part, protests and demonstrations during the early 1960s remained nonviolent. However, in the late 1960s, many groups grew tired of waiting for change. Anti-war demonstrations increasingly broke out into violence between protesters and law enforcement officials. Some anti-war groups began to use more aggressive, or militant, methods to achieve their goals.

The civil rights movements of various groups also took a more militant stand during this period. For example, a number of African Americans formed the Black Panthers to fight for rights. The Black Panthers used aggression to fulfill the group's mission.

The Chicano Movement was no different. In the beginning, El Movimiento was nonviolent. As time wore on, however, some Chicano leaders resorted to violence. In addition, demonstrators began to fight back in response to acts of police brutality. Peaceful demonstrations would often end in violence.

Give Us Back Our Land!

One Chicano group that started as a nonviolent organization was the Alianza Federal de las Mercedes (Federal Alliance of Land Grants) in New Mexico. Reies López Tijerina founded the Alianza in 1963. Tijerina was a fiery and effective preacher who felt deeply for his people. He decided that Chicanos should try to get back lands lost after the Mexican American War in 1848.

At first, Tijerina used legal arguments. He researched old documents and determined that many state park lands in New Mexico had belonged to Mexican Americans. The Treaty of Guadalupe-Hidalgo, which ended the Mexican American War, was supposed to guarantee the property of those families. But their land had been stolen by the state of New Mexico.

Through emotional speeches, Tijerina gave Mexican Americans hope that they would recover this land. The Alianza hired attorneys to present their cases. The people marched to the state capital in Albuquerque and appealed to the governor. Tijerina went to Washington, DC, to present his arguments. Yet, the government refused to take his requests seriously.

Frustrated, the Alianza responded by becoming more militant. Tijerina and the Alianza made several attempts to occupy land by force. During one attempt in May 1967, eight members of the Alianza were arrested. Tijerina then organized a raid on the courthouse where they were being held. Two officers were wounded during the assault. After this raid, the authorities harassed Tijerina and the Alianza.

Extreme militancy eventually became common in the land-grant movement. Tijerina was arrested and sentenced to several years in prison. In the end, the Alianza lost its battle to regain the lands. However, Tijerina's actions inspired many Chicanos who believed El Movimiento needed to become more aggressive in its struggle for justice.

Students for Justice

Chicano students were among those who were influenced by the efforts of Tijerina. A number of young Chicanos had already been active in the farm workers' movement. Now they wanted to be part of the changes they believed El Movimiento would bring.

One such change was an end to the racism students experienced in universities and high schools. In March 1968, Mexican American students in an East Los Angeles high school staged a walkout. Led by Sal Castro, a high school teacher, they protested poor treatment of Mexican American students. They complained that they were receiving a second-rate education. Within a week, the protests spread from one school to another. Some estimate that more than 15,000 students left their classes throughout the Los Angeles area.

High school students elsewhere also organized protests. In Texas, more than 30 school walkouts occurred between 1968 and the mid-1970s. In Colorado, a group of students at Denver's West High School demonstrated against racist remarks made by a teacher. They decided to get help from an organization called the Crusade for Justice. Founded by Rodolfo "Corky" Gonzales, this organization promoted equal rights for Chicanos. Gonzales addressed the students during their walkout. The protest lasted three days. Street riots broke out, and police attacked students with clubs and tear gas.

Even before the protests had broken out, Gonzales had been arranging a conference to bring together young Chicanos in Denver. Several days after the protests at West High School, Gonzales opened the First Chicano Youth Liberation Conference. Gonzales was well known among students. His epic poem "I am Joaquín" had become an anthem for El Movimiento. More than 1,000 young people attended the conference. They left energized and willing to continue the Chicano struggle.

Shortly after the conference, another group of students met at the University of California, Santa Barbara. Many of those students had been to the conference in Denver. They formed El Movimiento Estudiantil de Aztlán (MEChA, Aztlán Student Movement). MEChA succeeded in its goals to unite Chicano students and create Chicano studies programs in many universities.

The Brown Berets

In 1966, Vicky Castro was president of the Young Citizens for Community Action. The motto of this small group of Los Angeles students was "To serve, observe, protect." The purpose of this

During the early 1970s, Chicano high school students staged walkouts in California, Texas, and Colorado. The students were protesting discrimination in education. They wanted better schools, teachers, and classes.

group was to protect Mexican Americans against attack. Its members opened a coffeehouse for Chicano teenagers. The coffeehouse offered them a place to meet and talk. By then, David Sánchez had become president.

The police saw the coffeehouse as a threat only because many young Chicanos gathered there. Officers harassed the group and beat up David Sánchez. After this incident, the group became more militant. It changed its name to the Brown Berets, because the members all wore small brown hats. Soon other groups of Berets formed throughout California and in other states.

The Brown Berets joined with other groups, such as MEChA, to form the National Chicano Moratorium Committee, in 1969. A **moratorium** is a form of protest in which all work and school activity is stopped in order to bring about change. The committee was formed to protest the high percentage of Chicano casualties in the Vietnam War. Its leaders organized the August 29, 1970, march in Laguna Park that you read about earlier.

In Laguna Park, police clashed with the protesters. The results were horrible: almost 200 people were arrested, many were injured, and three were killed. Rubén Salazar, a respected

A Good Movie to See

Chicano! History of the Mexican American Civil Rights Movement. Episode 4: "Fighting for Political Power." Produced by the National Latino Communications Center and Galán Productions, Inc., in association with KCET/Los Angeles, 1996.

This video focuses on the birth of Mexican American political power and the creation of La Raza Unida, a third political party. It brings the Chicano Movement to life as young Chicanos struggle for equality.

journalist for the *Los Angeles Times* and manager of a Spanish-language TV station, was among those killed. He became a symbol for El Movimiento. Corky Gonzales of the Denver Crusade for Justice was among those arrested.

These clashes with police were not limited to Mexican American protests. African Americans, Native Americans, and anti-war protesters faced the same brutality in their struggles.

More Young Leaders

We no longer accept the fact that we are powerless and need to be complaining about our powerlessness. We know we're powerful, we know we can be organized, we know we can triumph.

The young man who made that statement was José Angel Gutiérrez. In 1967, Gutiérrez and four friends founded the Mexican American Youth Organization (MAYO). The goal of MAYO was to bring about social change in the Mexican American community and to train young Chicanos for leadership positions.

On the same day of Corky Gonzales's youth conference in Denver, Gutiérrez led a march of about 2,000 people in Del Rio, Texas. Two events had prompted the protest. A Chicano couple had been beaten by a Texas law officer. Also some Chicanos from Del Rio who protested the beating at the courthouse had been fired. This protest in Del Rio made MAYO very popular among Chicanos.

MAYO also helped students fight for justice. In the spring of 1969, high school students in Crystal City, Texas, protested against discrimination. Soon, the protest grew into a demand for **bilingual** education, or education in two languages: Spanish and English. The students also demanded better school buildings and an end to racist remarks by teachers.

About 1,700 students walked out of school. Their parents joined them in a school ban. Gutiérrez of MAYO was the organizing force behind them. The school ban lasted until the school board gave in to most of the demands. Chicanos in Crystal City tasted the success of organized protest. They were now ready to organize themselves into a political party.

A New Party

MAYO eventually became La Raza Unida, a new political party organized by Gutiérrez. The party was formed because the needs of Mexican Americans were not being met by either the Democratic or the Republican parties. La Raza Unida was founded in Texas in 1969. It quickly spread to other states, such as Colorado, California, Arizona, and New Mexico.

The main goal of La Raza Unida was to win elections and put more Chicanos in office. La Raza Unida won a number of victories, and at one time its members held a majority of the elected posts in Crystal City and Zavala County, Texas.

Putting people in office, however, was not the only goal. The idea was not only to win elections but also to educate Chicanos about politics. As one high school student put it,

We Chicanos have to vote for people who will help us. I mean, if there are candidates who will help us, we will be given more opportunities to get ahead in life.

Thinking It Over

1. Why did Reies López Tijerina believe that Mexican Americans were entitled to lands in New Mexico?

2. **Defending a Position** Reread the quote above from the high school student. Do you agree with the opinion that politicians can help shape one's future? Explain.

Active Learning: Make notes for your letter to the editor about the changes that took place in the Chicano Movement during the late 1960s and early 1970s. Note the names of organizations that were formed, their founders, purposes, and methods of protest.

3 The Chicano Movement Today

The Chicano Movement, like many civil rights movements of the 1960s, lost strength in the middle to late 1970s. Most of the Chicano groups and organizations that were created in the 1960s are gone. However, the **legacy** of the Chicano Movement continues. A legacy is something valuable that is handed down from an older generation to a younger generation.

The Struggle Goes On

Part of the legacy of the Chicano Movement is the Mexican American Legal Defense and Education Fund. Known as MALDEF, it was founded in San Antonio, Texas, in 1968. MALDEF is now a national organization that is dedicated to protecting and promoting the civil rights of Latinos in the United States.

MALDEF's staff includes over 20 attorneys. They defend cases that affect the rights of Latinos. Some of the cases MALDEF handles have to do with employment, education, immigration, political access, and language.

In the 1970s, Vilma Martínez helped MALDEF grow and gain prominence. Thanks to Martínez's persistence and dedication, MALDEF is today one of the most important legacies of El Movimiento.

A Legacy in Education

One focus of the Chicano Movement was the importance of education. In fact, Chicanos who attended or taught at universities helped to define much of the movement.

During and after the Chicano Movement, a number of Chicano Studies programs were established at universities throughout the Southwest. Such programs helped to preserve Chicano history and foster cultural understanding. The first Chicano Studies department in the nation was founded in 1968 at California State College, Los Angeles. The department was formed after Mexican American students staged protests. Soon, more Chicano Studies courses and departments were established.

Today, almost every university in the Southwest has a MEChA organization. MEChA has been responsible for developing and maintaining many Chicano studies programs.

A Political and Cultural Presence

MALDEF and La Raza Unida contributed to the political success of many Mexican Americans. Through the efforts of these groups, many Mexican Americans have been elected to public office. After La Raza Unida fell into decline in the late 1970s, many of its leaders became active in the Democratic party in Texas. A number were elected to the Texas legislature and at least one, Ciro Rodriguez, was elected to the U.S. Congress.

In recent years, Mexican Americans have played an important role in government. Among them, Henry Cisneros, the former mayor of San Antonio, is an example of a new breed of young Chicano political leaders. In the early 1990s, he was appointed U.S. Secretary of Housing and Urban Development by President Bill Clinton.

Mexican Americans also occupy important positions in organized labor today. Linda Chávez-Thompson has risen to top labor leadership positions, both in Texas and at the national level.

Another legacy of El Movimiento is the recognition of Chicano literature and arts. Mexican museums are now established in Chicago and San Francisco to preserve and display Mexican art. Amalia Mesa-Bains is a widely recognized artist and writer who has been involved in the Chicano artist movement since the 1960s. Luis Valdez, the founder of El Teatro Campesino, took his play *Zoot Suit* all the way to Broadway. The work of such artists enriches the lives of all Americans by exposing them to the Mexican American experience.

A Lasting Legacy

The Chicano Movement opened minds and doors, thus creating opportunities for Mexican Americans. It gave many Mexican Americans self-esteem and pride in their heritage that had not existed before. At one time, Mexican Americans were referred to as the "invisible minority." As a result of El Movimiento, that will never be said again.

Active Learning: Explain what the Chicano Movement accomplished in the 1960s and 1970s and what its goals are today.

Thinking It Over

1. What gains have Chicanos made in government?
2. **Forecasting** What could be some future goals of Mexican Americans? Identify and explain at least one goal they might want to achieve.

GOING TO THE SOURCE

From "Are You a Chicano?"

In the 1960s and 1970s, many young Mexican Americans began to call themselves *Chicanos*. In a 1972 newsletter published by the D-Q University in Davis, California, a writer discusses what it means to use this term.

. . . Many of us prefer to call ourselves Chicanos because it reflects our feeling for our culture and heritage, our pride in who we are and where we came from, and it gives us a sense of unity. But that's not all the term means; besides unity it has brought suspicion and has tended to separate the "Chicanos" from many others of Mexican descent through a misunderstanding of the term, the way it is used, and each other.

Lately, Chicano has been used as a kind of measuring stick. This has served to split us into groups based solely on what we choose to call ourselves. That we are wasting our time and energy arguing among ourselves about what name we should go under is just one of the problems raised by this "hang-up" of ours. What difference does it make?

Some of the time it seems that many of us forget that we are a very diverse group of *individuals*. Many of us don't know the field, the barrios, the Spanish language, or even the pronunciation of our own names. This might not be the way we would like it to be, but that's the way it is. These things are nobody's fault, they just happened and we should be ready to go from there . . .

The major "virtue" that we lack is patience. Apparently it's been too long for some of us to remember that all of us didn't always have the pride in La Raza we have now . . . It's time that we all brought each other along and took the time to explain to each other our pride and our feelings about what we're doing.

The problems of education, housing, unemployment, etc., are still there waiting to be solved by Chicanos, Mexicans, Mexican-Americans, Latinos—in short, anyone who sincerely wants to do the work. So it's not a matter of what you call yourself— if you want to help, DO IT! And you'll be whatever you want to be, and be called whatever you want to be called.

From Dorothy and Thomas Hoobler,
The Mexican American Family Album,
Oxford University Press, 1994, p. 104

1. According to the writer, what effect does the use of the term *Chicano* sometimes have on the Mexican American community?

2. **Formulating Opinions** According to the writer, what should be the main concerns of Chicanos? Do you agree or disagree with this position? Explain your answers.

Case Study Review

Identifying Main Ideas

1. What were the goals of El Movimiento?
2. In what ways did students participate in the Chicano Movement? Give at least one example of a student demonstration and explain what it accomplished.
3. How does MALDEF protect the civil rights of Mexican Americans and other Latinos?

Working Together

Work with a partner. Choose one Chicano leader or political figure that you read about in this case study. Use library resources to research that person's life. Then write a two-page biography. Make sure you define the leader's goals and accomplishments.

Active Learning

Writing a Letter to the Editor Review the notes you took as you read this case study. Then look at copies of your local newspaper and read some letters to the editor. You will see that letters to the editor express the writer's opinion about a particular topic. Next, imagine that it is the anniversary of the march that occurred in Los Angeles in August 1970. Write a letter to the editor of your local paper explaining what the Chicano Movement was, what its goals were, and whether you think any of those goals have been achieved.

Lessons for Today

Discuss the methods Chicanos used in the 1960s and 1970s to fight for their civil rights. Are some of those methods still used today? Think of something you would like to improve in your school or community. What have you learned from the Chicano Movement that could help you bring the change you want to your school or community?

What Might You Have Done?

Imagine that you are a member of Tijerina's Alianza. You have made several legal attempts to regain lands that belonged to your ancestors before the Mexican American War of 1848. Some members of the Alianza want to take the land by force. How would you convince them to use other, peaceful methods?

Determining Cause and Effect

Causes and Effects: Key Words

Certain words can give you a clue to recognizing causes and effects. The following words may indicate a cause:

■ since

■ because of

■ due to

The following words may indicate an effect:

■ therefore

■ as a result

The Chicano Movement was a major occurrence in the history of Mexican Americans. As you have read, a number of events happened within the context of the Chicano Movement. Each of these events had both causes and effects. Causes are events or conditions that produce an event. They explain why the event happened. Effects are events or conditions that the major event caused. They explain what happened as a result of the event.

Use the graphic organizer below to study the causes and effects of the August 1970 Chicano march. Then read the list of events below. In your notebook, write at least one cause and one effect of each event.

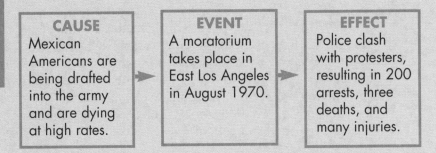

CAUSE	EVENT	EFFECT
Mexican Americans are being drafted into the army and are dying at high rates.	A moratorium takes place in East Los Angeles in August 1970.	Police clash with protesters, resulting in 200 arrests, three deaths, and many injuries.

EVENTS

1. César Chávez fights for the rights of migrant farm workers.

2. Reies López Tijerina and the Alianza try to get back lost lands in New Mexico.

3. Chicano students are drawn to El Movimiento.

4. The First Chicano Youth Liberation Conference takes place in Denver in 1969.

5. The Young Citizens for Community Action becomes the Brown Berets.

MELA: THE MOTHERS OF EAST LOS ANGELES

The Mothers of East Lost Angeles protested the building of another prison in their community. This was just the start of many of MELA's efforts to protect their community.

CRITICAL QUESTIONS

- Why did mothers in East Los Angeles unite to protect their neighborhood?
- What strategies did the Mothers of East Los Angeles use in their fight to save their neighborhood?

TERMS TO KNOW

- barrio
- coalition
- grassroots
- lobby
- incinerator
- toxic
- immunization

ACTIVE LEARNING

In this case study, you will learn about a group of mothers who formed an organization to protect their neighborhood's environment. At the end of the case study, you will prepare a two-minute speech about one of the issues you have read about. Throughout the case study, there are Active Learning hint boxes. Use the suggestions in the hint boxes to help you prepare your assignment.

It was May 1985. A small group of women sat waiting in Juana Gutiérrez's living room. They wondered why California State Assemblywoman Gloria Molina had called them together. The group of women lived in the neighborhood of Boyle Heights, a mostly Mexican American **barrio,** or neighborhood, located right next to East Los Angeles. Finally, Molina arrived and began to explain why she had wanted to meet with them. The governor of California had just approved plans for the construction of a sixth prison in East Los Angeles. The proposed prison was to be built right in their neighborhood.

The women were outraged. They all believed that the site proposed for the prison was unsuitable. More than 30 schools and thousands of houses stood within two miles of the planned prison site. In addition, the state had approved the plan without discussing it with members of the Boyle Heights community. California policy required community feedback *before* selecting a prison site. The people of Boyle Heights felt betrayed.

Molina finished explaining the prison plan to the group. Then she turned to them and said, "Now you know the problem. What are you going to do about it?"

1 The Mothers of East Los Angeles Unite

Juana Gutiérrez and the other women vowed to defeat the prison plan. For more than 10 years, they had worked hard to make Boyle Heights a safe community. They were not about to allow the state to build yet another prison so close to their homes and schools. A prison would endanger the safety of their neighborhood.

To the people of Boyle Heights, it seemed like another example of racism. They believed the state would never have made these plans for an Anglo, or white, neighborhood.

East Los Angeles had its fair share of prisons. As Gutiérrez's husband Ricardo put it, "We don't need a prison here. We need jobs and better schools."

A Leader in the Community

Juana Gutiérrez was a leader in the Boyle Heights community long before the prison issue arose. In the 1970s, Gutiérrez had organized a Neighborhood Watch program. This group's aim was to oust gangs from Boyle Heights. The program succeeded in practically ridding Boyle Heights of gangs and drugs.

It seemed natural that Gutiérrez would be a leader in the fight against the planned prison. When Assemblywoman Molina heard about the prison issue, she immediately called Gutiérrez. Gutiérrez gathered all her Neighborhood Watch captains at her house. This was the beginning of MELA—The Mothers of East Los Angeles.

Getting Involved

Gutiérrez's decision to stand up to the government of California was a good example of how she had led her life. She believed that people must fight for what they believe in.

Born in rural Mexico, Juana moved to Ciudad Juárez on the border of El Paso, Texas, with her parents in 1942. Juana was then in her twenties. Her parents were very cautious about getting involved in their new community. They warned their daughter not to get mixed up in controversial issues. But Gutiérrez did not agree with their attitude.

In 1954, Juana married Ricardo Gutiérrez, a Mexican American and a U.S. Marine. The couple moved to Boyle Heights and have lived there ever since. Together, they raised nine children.

Their children were the reason Juana Gutiérrez first became involved in her community. She wanted to be sure that they would be safe at school and free of harm when playing outside.

Juana Gutiérrez, a founder of MELA, and her husband (in front) have lived in this house for over 40 years. Together they have fought to protect and improve their community for their children and future generations.

She joined the Parent-Teacher Association (PTA) of her children's school and became an active member. Both Juana and Ricardo Gutiérrez believed strongly in the value of education. They encouraged their children to finish high school. All of their children attended college.

Fighting for the Children

Soon after Assemblywoman Molina's visit, Aurora Castillo joined the group of women fighting the prison. Like the others, she was outraged. Castillo's interest in community activities was rooted in her family's values. Her family had lived in California for five generations—"from before the Anglos discovered it," she says.

From a young age, Castillo's father encouraged her to get involved. "Put your shoulders back, hold your head high, be proud of your heritage," he told Aurora and his other children. Her parents encouraged her to work toward her dreams. Castillo attended business school and worked at Douglas Aircraft Company during World War II.

Like Gutiérrez, Castillo became involved in the Boyle Heights community. She once explained:

> *The mother is the soul of the family, but the child is the heartbeat. We fight to keep the heart of our community beating. Not just for our children, but for everyone's children.*

Fighting Against the Prison

Juana Gutiérrez, Aurora Castillo, and the other women founded a group called the Mothers of East Los Angeles (MELA). Although MELA was created to fight against the prison, it would deal with many other community issues in the years to come.

The members of MELA immediately set to work protesting against the planned prison. First, the women got in touch with everyone they knew in the neighborhood. They rang doorbells and made telephone calls. Members addressed the community in churches after Sunday mass. They held meetings and distributed information. Before long, the group had grown in size to several hundred members.

To increase its power, MELA joined with about 30 other community groups to form a group called "The Coalition against the Prison." A **coalition** (koh-uh-LIH-shun) is an alliance of many groups that are fighting for or against a single issue. The coalition made MELA stronger than it would have been alone.

Weekly Marches

Members of the coalition knew they had to bring the prison issue to the attention of the public. They decided to organize weekly candlelight marches through the neighborhood. These marches publicized the issue of the planned prison. They also attracted the attention of television stations and newspapers.

Every Monday evening the women wore white kerchiefs and held candles as they marched over a bridge near the proposed prison site. Gutiérrez explained that the white kerchiefs represented MELA's commitment to non-violence.

The marches were a great success. They attracted thousands of people. Television stations showed up to broadcast the story to millions of viewers. Mexican American leaders such as César Chávez came to march with the mothers. The largest of the Monday marches attracted 3,500 people.

A Grassroots Organization

The fight against the prison would be difficult, but MELA would not be defeated. One of MELA's strengths was that it was a **grassroots** organization, an organization that is run by local people. Because such groups are usually small organizations with strong local support, they can often respond quickly and efficiently to local issues. For example, Juana Gutiérrez explained

The Mothers of East Los Angeles used many different strategies to fight against the construction of a prison in their neighborhood. One strategy was to join a coalition.

how she and her husband went to neighborhood churches to gather support against the prison. She said:

> On one Sunday alone, my husband Ricardo and I gathered 900 signatures [of persons who opposed construction of the prison in East Los Angeles] among the parishioners of Santa Isabel and Saint Mary's churches.

MELA and the coalition also gained the support of those outside the community. Television coverage and growing membership in the coalition helped spread the word. This made it especially hard for California's government to ignore the issue.

All the Way to Sacramento

MELA used other means to tell state lawmakers and the governor how it felt about the prison. To get the governor's attention, MELA would find out when he was speaking near Los Angeles. Then MELA members would show up with protest signs that got the attention of the press. The governor's staff was annoyed at these activities. But the publicity about the prison forced the governor to respond to the issue.

On a number of occasions, the group organized trips to Sacramento, the capital of California. MELA members worked to **lobby**, or to try to influence, their state lawmakers. The members of MELA were not experienced at lobbying. They felt nervous about approaching the legislators. Aurora Castillo recalled the group's first trip to Sacramento:

> We approached the first news conference on the Capitol steps hungry and worn out. Then, one of our Latino legislators turned to us and said, "This is your state capital. You have every right to be here."

The members of MELA also had knowledge on their side. They had studied the issue carefully and knew what they wanted. Ricardo Gutiérrez remembered that the legislators were very surprised that a group of mothers from East Los Angeles knew so much about the laws. He said:

> They were expecting that once [the mothers] would be asked a question, they would not know how to answer. Every question they were asked, the Mothers of East Los Angeles had answers for.

The 350-mile trips to Sacramento were expensive. MELA and the other members of the coalition held fund-raisers. They had breakfasts, dinners, and dances to raise money. A local bus company donated the buses to take them on trips. It was a difficult struggle, but MELA members knew that they had to fight to win.

Thinking It Over

1. Why did Gloria Molina call the women of Boyle Heights together?
2. **Comparing and Contrasting** Compare Juana Gutiérrez's family to Aurora Castillo's. How did each woman's parents feel about getting involved in community affairs?

Active Learning: You have just read about the attempt to build another prison in Boyle Heights and about how MELA began to fight it. Take notes on the reasons why MELA was opposed to the prison site. You may wish to write about these reasons in your speech.

2 Protecting the Environment

The fight against the new prison took seven long years. During that time, the members of MELA dealt with a number of other threats to their neighborhood.

When MELA found out that officials were going to allow an incinerator to be built close to their neighborhood, they swung into action. Here, 200 people marched on Downey Avenue to protest the incinerator. In the end, MELA and the coalition were successful.

A Pipeline Proposal

In 1987, MELA found out about a proposal to build a pipeline through East Los Angeles. The pipeline would carry oil from one point along the California coastline to another. Instead of building the pipeline along the coastline, the company building the pipeline chose to take a 20-mile detour inland. This detour routed the pipeline right through East Los Angeles.

Building along the coastline would mean a shorter and less expensive pipeline. Why didn't the planners choose to build along the coastline? Mainly, they wanted to avoid the wealthy communities located there. The builders knew that these communities would fight against the pipeline. The builders decided to run the pipeline through the poor neighborhoods of East Los Angeles—even near a few schools.

The oil company executives hoped that the residents of East Los Angeles would not find out about the pipeline until it was built. They did not count on MELA getting involved.

MELA again led the coalition of community groups to fight against the pipeline. The coalition pointed out that the pipeline was being laid only three feet underground. If the pipeline ever burst, it would mean disaster for their community. The coalition successfully battled against the effort to lay the pipeline through East Los Angeles.

Toxic Waste

In 1986, the group found out that the state planned to build a hazardous waste **incinerator** in Vernon, a small industrial city near Boyle Heights. An incinerator is a large furnace that burns trash. The proposed incinerator would burn **toxic**, or poisonous, trash. Its builders planned it to be the largest incinerator of its kind.

MELA and other community groups believed that the incinerator would blow cancer-causing materials into the air. They argued that the incinerator would also create thousands of tons of toxic ash that would have to be buried somewhere. Juana Gutiérrez pointed out that the incinerator would be "burning hospital trash and other toxic things . . . right here in our community. That's too close to the schools and the churches."

Again, MELA formed a coalition. This time the coalition included national organizations concerned with protecting the environment. The members of MELA again made telephone calls and used local churches to let people know what was going on. The coalition organized a number of protests against the incinerator. One demonstration attracted more than 1,000 people. The coalition also fought in court to halt plans for the incinerator.

Active Learning: Whether or not to build the pipeline or the incinerator would make good topics for a speech. If you choose one of these topics, review this section and take notes on the issue.

Other Victories for the Community

In May 1991, MELA learned that the plans to build the incinerator had been dropped. The years of hard work had paid off. Members of MELA and the coalition gathered together to celebrate victory. They stood on the site that had been planned for the waste incinerator. "We chased them out," declared one protester.

The following year, the state decided not to build the prison. The Mothers of East Los Angeles and all the other coalition members had won. The victory had not come easily. Yet, they had proved that a community that works together can accomplish nearly anything.

Dedicated Latina Politicians

The members of MELA worked hard to fight against the prison, incinerator, and pipeline. Often, they battled against elected leaders who seemed not to care about the residents of East Los Angeles. A number of elected officials, however, did care and helped a great deal. Two of them were Gloria Molina and Lucille Roybal-Allard.

As you read at the start of this case study, Assemblywoman Gloria Molina told the Boyle Heights community about the proposed prison. Molina, the daughter of Mexican immigrants, won election to the state assembly in 1982. She was the first Mexican American woman to sit in California's Assembly. In 1987, Molina won a seat on the Los Angeles City Council. Then in 1991, she was elected to the powerful Board of Supervisors in Los Angeles county. As the first Mexican American to sit on the board since 1875, Molina has earned a place in history. Despite Molina's rise in politics, she did not forget the people who voted her into office. In 1992, when the prison proposal was defeated, she declared:

> *This victory leaves the community with the confidence that there is power . . . . Now it can just translate for every other issue: More schools, more jobs and a safer community.*

When Gloria Molina left the assembly, Lucille Roybal-Allard, another Mexican American woman, took her place. Roybal-Allard grew up in Boyle Heights. Her father, Ed Roybal, was a member of the U.S. House of Representatives. Roybal-Allard helped MELA get its message to other elected officials in Sacramento. She supported the group through its struggles. Then in 1992, Roybal-Allard was elected to the U.S. House of Representatives.

3 The Work Continues

MELA is often asked to join other groups in their protests and to train members of other local organizations. In their efforts to train people, the members of MELA stress knowledge of the issues as a key to success. They explain that it is important that the residents of a community really understand the issues they are protesting.

Taking the Offensive

MELA has won many battles in its fight to make East Los Angeles a safe community. However, its members know that there is much more work to do. They continue to fight against plans that threaten their neighborhood's environment. They have gone one step beyond defending against prisons and incinerators.

MELA runs a number of programs to help the residents of East Los Angeles, including programs to fight water waste, lead poisoning, and lack of educational opportunities.

One of its more successful programs deals with water conservation. The program not only conserves water. It also recycles materials and brings jobs into the community. MELA has hired members of the community to install special water-saving toilets. Between 1992 and 1994, MELA installed over 32,000 of these toilets. Elsa López, Gutiérrez's daughter, runs this program. She explains that the old toilets are recycled, or used again. They are "crushed and mixed with old tires, which are used for roadways to cover potholes and for freeways damaged by earthquakes."

MELA also runs an **immunization** program. Immunization makes a person's body able to resist certain illnesses. MELA's program informs parents about the injections their children need. Members of MELA help bring children to clinics to get these injections. To help prevent lead poisoning in children, MELA distributes information and helps parents bring their children in for testing.

MELA's scholarship program gives money to high school and college students. The money is given to students who need financial aid and who also show a desire to help the community. Rosie Vasquez, a high school graduate, said that her goal was to set up a pediatric practice in East Los Angeles. Vasquez was one of more than 30 students who received scholarships to help with college tuition and expenses in 1995.

A Good Book to Read

Women Reshaping Human Rights, by Marguerite Guzman Bouvard. Wilmington, DE: SR Books, 1996.

Each chapter of Bouvard's book contains the story of a woman activist. Chapter 10 is the story of Juana Gutiérrez and MELA. The story of MELA is told in the words of Gutiérrez, her husband, and one of the couple's daughters.

Building Community Spirit

Leaders of MELA have been honored for their hard work. Several have won awards for their service to the community and the environment.

Juana Gutiérrez has been honored for her leadership. In 1994, she won the Citizen of the Year Award of the National Association for Bilingual Education. In 1995, President Bill Clinton honored Gutiérrez and MELA at a White House ceremony.

Aurora Castillo won the 1995 Goldman Environmental Prize. At $75,000, it is the most valuable environmental prize in the world. In accepting the prize, Castillo said simply that all people, regardless of where they live or who they are, "have a right to a clean environment."

Both Castillo and Gutiérrez agree that the awards mean little when compared with the work they do in their community. MELA's work has sent a message to California's government: East Los Angeles is not a dumping ground for unwanted projects. It is a community that will fight for its rights.

In order to keep the work going, MELA has encouraged younger people to take active roles in the community. Due in part to MELA's efforts, many young people have returned to the neighborhood. Lucy Ramos, one of the founding members of MELA, put it this way:

> The politicians thought we wouldn't fight, but we united and said, "Ya basta, enough." This [is] a dumping ground no more. . . . The kids around here were babies when we started. Now they too will fight for what they believe in because we showed them their voices count.

Thinking It Over

1. How does the water conservation program help residents of East Los Angeles?
2. **Analyzing** Why do you think MELA began to raise money for scholarships?

Since successfully battling against the prison, the incinerator, and other environmental issues, MELA has become a force for change in East Los Angeles. MELA has taken many steps to help the residents of their neighborhood, such as running recycling programs and giving scholarships to community youth.

GOING TO THE SOURCE

A Letter to the Editor

After Juana Gutiérrez received word about the defeat of the toxic waste incinerator in Vernon, she wrote the following letter to the *Los Angeles Times*.

Vernon Victory

The Mothers of East Los Angeles at Santa Isabel would like to express their gratitude to the California community for its support against the Vernon toxic waste incinerator. On May 24, the *Times* reported that Security Environmental Systems abandoned its project to build our state's first such incinerator.

This victory would not have been possible without the support of Assemblywoman Lucille Roybal-Allard, state Sen. [Senator] Art Torres and U.S. Rep. [Representative] Edward Roybal. Through their efforts, environmental groups such as Greenpeace and community groups from environmentally threatened cities such as Santa Maria, Casmalia, Kettleman City, Rosamont and Martinez joined together to halt this unproven technology. Along with community groups from South-Central Los Angeles, this unprecedented [never before seen] coalition united to work for the betterment of California's future.

It is no secret that chemical- and toxin-producing corporations looking to make a fast dollar target communities of color because of their stereotypical powerlessness. Through this victory, let it be known that communities of color throughout the state of California will unite whenever children are threatened.

Juana Beatriz Gutiérrez, President, Mothers of East Los Angeles
From *Los Angeles Times*, June 24, 1991, p. B-4.

1. With which other communities did MELA form a coalition to fight the building of the incinerator?
2. **Analyzing** Why does Gutiérrez believe that East Los Angeles was chosen for the site of the incinerator?

Case Study Review

Identifying Main Ideas

1. Why did Juana Gutiérrez and the women who formed MELA object to the proposed prison site in East Los Angeles?

2. Give two examples that show how MELA attracted the attention of media such as television and newspapers.

3. What programs has MELA begun to help the community in East Los Angeles?

Working Together

Form a group with two or three classmates. Use library resources to find out more about grassroots organizations. One organization you may wish to study is COPS (Communities Organized for Public Services). This San Antonio organization has been a model for other organizations throughout the Southwest. After you have completed your research, make a presentation to the class about grassroots organizations. Provide examples of these organizations. Also, discuss the pros and cons of a grassroots organization.

Active Learning

Making a Speech Review the notes you took while reading this case study. Imagine that you have been asked by MELA to give a speech before California's state assembly about an issue in this case study. First outline your speech and then write a first draft. After you have rewritten your draft, read your speech to the class.

Lessons for Today

As you have read, the women of Boyle Heights worked together to improve the environment of their community. Look through your local newspapers and, if possible, talk to residents in your neighborhood. What would you like to see changed in your community environment? What can you do to make these changes possible?

What Might You Have Done?

Imagine that your neighborhood was threatened with the construction of a prison, an incinerator, or a pipeline. How would you inform your neighbors of the threat to the community environment? Would you use some of the same methods as MELA? Can you think of other peaceful ways to fight the issue?

CRITICAL THINKING | Examining Issues and Making Decisions

Why Volunteer?

According to one survey, American teens are ready to take action even if it means making personal sacrifices.

Volunteers say that they get involved for practical reasons. But what they get out of volunteering is something else. They feel good about themselves, get to know themselves better, feel "empowered" (not helpless), feel they are part of life rather than observers of it, and feel happy doing something that they choose to do.

The Mothers of East Los Angeles believe in getting young people in their neighborhood involved in community service. Sometimes, they pay teenagers for the work they do, but at other times they ask the teens to **volunteer**.

When people volunteer, they donate time to a cause. Teenage volunteers play an important role in their communities. In many cases, young people run recycling programs, staff soup kitchens, clean school yards and parks, keep senior citizens company, and much, much more. Across the United States, teens give aid to those who need help.

If you wanted to volunteer, how would you choose which organization to work for? To make a wise decision, you would need to examine certain issues. For example, do you want to work directly with people in need? Or would you be happier behind the scenes, helping out in an office, writing a newsletter, or organizing money-raising events?

The questions below will help you think about becoming a volunteer. Read the questions and answer them on a separate sheet of paper.

1. (a) What are three activities that I enjoy doing?
   (b) What are three activities that I don't enjoy doing?

2. What is an activity that I've never done before but have always wanted to do?

3. What do I want to gain from volunteering?

4. Of all the problems that I see or hear about, which ones bother me most?

Think about your responses. Write a paragraph about the type of volunteer activity you would most like to do.

Foreign-owned factories in Mexico are called maquiladoras. Most are located on the U.S.-Mexican border. The worker in the maquiladora shown here assembles televisions.

TRADE ACROSS THE BORDER

CRITICAL QUESTIONS

- How does trade between the United States and Mexico affect each nation's economy?
- How does NAFTA affect the people of Mexico and the United States?

TERMS TO KNOW

- maquiladoras
- tariffs
- colonias
- NAFTA
- free trade

ACTIVE LEARNING

In this case study, you will be reading about factories that are located near the U.S.-Mexican border and about trade between the United States and Mexico. When you have completed this case study, you will work with a classmate to write questions for a mock interview with a Mexican factory worker. As you read, look for Active Learning boxes to help you take notes for your interview.

María Luna lives in Reynosa, a city in Mexico just a few miles from Brownsville, Texas. She assembles, or puts together, seat belts at a factory. Once they are assembled, the seat belts are sent back to the United States. Her weekly take-home earnings amount to about $31 in U.S. money. That may not sound like a good salary to people in the United States. However, it is probably twice as much money as she would earn back home in the city of Veracruz on the gulf coast of Mexico.

After María sent word of her increased earnings to her family in Veracruz, a couple of nieces arrived in Reynosa to join her. Conditions are not always good in the factory. María and her nieces work long hours. There is a housing shortage, and pollution is on the rise. Yet these women have found better jobs and higher wages in the factory than in most other places in Mexico.

1 Factories on the Border

Like María and her nieces, people in many other families are joining the growing population of Reynosa. They are part of an industrial boom in northern Mexico. Other Mexican cities along the border, such as Ciudad Juárez, Tijuana, Nuevo Laredo, and Matamoros, are also experiencing similar growth. (See the map on page 110.)

The seat belt factory where María works is typical of those in industries growing along the U.S.-Mexican border. Other border factories assemble products that you might find around your home or school. Such products include computer keyboards, TV monitors, and clothing. The border factories are called **maquiladoras** (mah-KEEL-uh-DOH-rahs).

What Is a Maquiladora?

A maquiladora is a foreign-owned factory in Mexico. U.S. firms own over half of these factories, either in whole or in part. Other maquiladoras are owned by Japan and other countries. The factories assemble imported parts, or parts that are shipped into Mexico. These factories then export, or send out, a finished product.

The U.S.-owned maquiladoras are usually located in Mexico near the U.S.-Mexican border. They often have a sister factory on the U.S. side of the border. This sister factory sends parts or raw materials to the maquiladora for assembly. Then it receives the assembled product from the maquiladora.

The first maquiladoras were typically electronic or clothing factories. Workers did assembly-line piece work. More recently, maquiladoras have varied from plant nurseries to chicken-processing plants. Eighty percent of the nearly 1,600 maquiladoras are located in three of the five northern states of Mexico: Chihuahua, Tamaulipas, and Baja California. Chihuahua and Tamaulipas border Texas. Baja California borders California. Of these three Mexican states, Chihuahua is the one with the largest number of maquiladora workers.

Maquiladoras and Mexico's Economy

Maquiladoras have existed in Mexico since the 1960s. The Mexican government decided to begin the program as part of a larger plan to boost the country's economy.

In Mexico, unemployment and rapid population growth have often been big challenges. At times, the unemployment rate has been as high as 50 percent. Mexico hoped that the maquiladoras would provide jobs and bring money into the country.

In some ways, the maquiladoras have lived up to Mexico's hopes. Border factories are an important source of jobs in Mexico. In 1996, employment rose by over 20 percent. Border factories provided jobs to more than 600,000 people.

Benefits for Workers

Workers at maquiladoras receive a number of benefits. César de la Rosa, a 26-year-old foreman in an appliance repair plant in Ciudad Juárez, points out some of these benefits. As an employee in a maquiladora, de la Rosa is a member of Mexico's social security system. This system offers low-cost medical care and home loans at special rates. As a member, de la Rosa has five days of paid vacation a year.

When Mexico began its maquiladora program, it hoped its workers would learn new job skills in the factories. Some of these hopes were realized. The maquiladoras do provide jobs, but they are not very high-paying or skilled jobs. Critics of the program argue that maquiladoras are run by non-Mexicans. Management positions are usually filled by people from the United States. Mexican law allows this. However, the law also requires that all hourly employees be Mexican. This is a way of guaranteeing that maquiladoras will employ many Mexican workers.

Arturo Arriaga is one of those who has benefited from working at a maquiladora. Arriaga, a 23-year-old employee of a steel company in Monterrey, Mexico, takes part in a training program sponsored by his employer. Since taking part in the program, his pay has nearly doubled to $13.38 a day. Arriaga is also eligible for regular promotions. He says that if he emigrated, or moved, to the United States, he might make more money at a lower-level job. However, Arriaga does not plan to move. As he explains, "Here I have a real career."

Drawbacks for Women Workers

Although employees in the maquiladoras do receive some benefits, there are some drawbacks to working in the factories.

The majority of workers in maquiladoras are women. The average age of these women workers is 23. Women who work at maquil-adoras earn money needed by their families. Yet most maquiladoras do not provide child care for working mothers. Mothers with older relatives nearby may leave young children in their care. In other cases, older brothers and sisters may need to stay home from school to care for a younger child. This means that the older children in the family do not receive a proper education.

Working conditions at some maquiladoras threaten the health of women workers and their children. At these factories, workers often come into contact with toxic, or poisonous, chemicals. Some researchers believe that there is a link between exposure to the chemicals by women workers and a rise in birth defects in their children.

The employment of women also affects the traditional family structure in Mexico. Typically, young women would have stayed at home to raise their families. Now, many spend a large part of the day working and commuting. For instance, Ana Serratos works at a maquiladora in Ciudad Juárez. She must get up every morning at 4 A.M. and endure two long bus rides to arrive at work at 7 A.M. She needs the work but earns only 35 cents an hour. Serratos remarks, "These companies from the United States and Japan don't pay people what they ought to." Her older sister, Leticia, comments: "Look how you have to suffer to earn a few pennies!"

Despite the drawbacks, the families of these women rely on the money that they earn. This money helps put food on the table for their families. Some women work in the factories to allow other family members to stay in school and to make sure that their families have health care.

Active Learning: Imagine that you are going to interview either María Luna, César de la Rosa, Ana Serratos, or her sister Leticia. Write down the questions you would ask this person during an interview.

Most workers in maquiladoras are women. For many of these women, a lack of child care is a serious concern. Some women, such as the one pictured here, take their children to work when school is not in session.

Advantages for the United States

At one time, many of the U.S. companies that now have maquiladoras in Mexico had factories in distant countries in Asia. There are several reasons why U.S. firms have set up factories in Mexico. First, they found that they can pay lower wages in Mexico and therefore make products at a lower cost.

Another advantage is that the location of Mexico on the U.S. border allows U.S. companies to save on transportation costs. For every maquiladora on the Mexican side, there is usually a warehousing operation on the U.S. side.

In addition, the environmental laws in Mexico are less strict than those in the United States. This means that U.S. companies do not have to spend money on expensive equipment to control pollution. More recently, however, Mexico has strengthened its environmental laws. Maquiladoras will need to observe these laws.

Although the maquiladoras have existed for over 30 years, it was not until the early 1980s that changes in Mexican laws encouraged their growth. One of these new laws eliminated **tariffs** on imported materials and parts. Tariffs are taxes that a government charges on goods that are imported from another country. Without tariffs and other restrictions, U.S. companies are now able to send materials back and forth across the border more cheaply.

Immigration Across the Border

There is another reason that some people in the United States support the growth of maquiladoras. Many supporters believe that these factory jobs may help decrease the flow of undocumented workers coming to the United States in search of work. However, the potential for work has attracted many Mexicans to the border cities. Not all of them find jobs when they arrive. Some of these people may then be tempted to cross into the United States illegally.

The search for work is the main reason Mexicans emigrate to the United States. As you have read, Mexico's unemployment rate is high. As many as 700,000 new workers enter the workforce in Mexico each year. Yet there are only about 300,000 new jobs for them. A number of unemployed Mexicans risk a move to the United States in hopes of finding work.

Since the 1960s, the number of Mexican immigrants in the United States has increased steadily. Immigrants with little money may come as migrant farm workers. Others may search for different types of work. Mexican immigrants often take low-paying jobs that require hard work and long hours. However, in these jobs, they earn more money than they would have in Mexico. Sometimes middle-class or wealthy Mexicans emigrate to escape the weak Mexican economy. Mexicans with money may invest in businesses or may have the education to get better-paying jobs in the United States.

Moving to the United States is not easy for Mexicans or for immigrants from most other countries. The United States uses a system of quotas, which limits the number of people who can move to the country each year. Because the quota system makes it so difficult to emigrate to the United States, a number of Mexicans choose to cross the border illegally. They enter the United States as undocumented immigrants and find whatever work they can.

A Good Movie to See

Bill Moyers's *A World of Ideas: Carlos Fuentes*, PBS Video, 1988.

Watch this interview and you will gain insight into the complex relationship between the United States and Mexico. Bill Moyers interviews well-known Mexican novelist and essayist Carlos Fuentes. The two men discuss the cultures and economies of the United States and Mexico, and how increased contact between the two helps both countries.

Thinking It Over

1. What is one benefit maquiladoras bring to Mexico? What is one disadvantage?
2. **Analyzing** If you lived in Mexico, what would encourage you to find a job at a maquiladora? What would discourage you?

2 The Border Economy

The economies of the United States and Mexico are closely linked. The United States is Mexico's largest trading partner. About two-thirds of Mexico's imports are purchased from the United States. About two-thirds of Mexico's exports go to the United States.

The income from the maquiladoras is important to the U.S and Mexican economies. This is especially true along the U.S.-Mexican border. Along the 2,000 mile stretch of border, a "border economy" has developed.

Sister Cities

At the International Bridge in Brownsville, Texas, you can see the border economy in action. The bridge links the cities of Brownsville and Matamoros, which is in Mexico. Arriving from both directions, hundreds of tractor-trailers wait their turn to cross the bridge. The tractor-trailers headed to Mexico carry tons of machine tools, car parts, computers, and factory equipment. The trucks making their way to the United States bring large quantities of Mexican-made machinery, electronic products, foods, and clothing from Matamoros into Texas.

Such intense trade between Brownsville and its sister city of Matamoros has made these cities part of one of the fastest growing areas along the U.S.-Mexican border.

Other sister cities along the U.S.-Mexican border have experienced similar growth. A few of these are Laredo-Nuevo Laredo, El Paso-Ciudad Juárez, and San Diego-Tijuana.

These sister cities depend on each other—and on the maquiladoras—for growth. The maquiladoras have contributed to the tremendous growth of the cities on the Mexican side of the border. They attract thousands of

U.S. visitors a year. Tourists from El Paso go down to *Plaza de las Américas* in Ciudad Juárez in search of bargains and a variety of Mexican goods. Visitors from Laredo, Texas, visit Nuevo Laredo, Mexico, to enjoy its restaurants, shopping areas, and night life.

From the Mexican side of the border, Mexican workers come to the United States to shop in malls. According to one estimate, Mexicans spend 40 to 60 percent of all the wages they earn on the U.S. side of the border. Stores in the U.S. border towns depend on business from Mexican customers. The increased income has created jobs in towns like Laredo and El Paso, Texas.

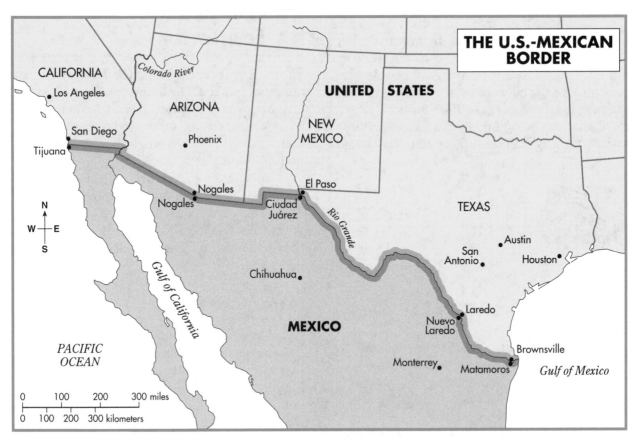

A number of cities along the U.S.-Mexican border are called sister cities. These cities, which lie across the border from one another, are economically linked. What is the U.S. sister city of Matamoros, Mexico? Which two sister cities are located on the California border?

Border Life

Along with the successes, the maquiladoras have caused a number of problems, especially for those who live on the Mexican side of the border. One very big problem is overcrowding. Hope for employment has brought thousands of Mexicans to the border.

The arrival of large numbers of workers causes overpopulation and a housing shortage. Workers have built **colonias** to ease the housing shortage. Colonias are poor neighborhoods where residents live in shacks made mostly of plywood and corrugated tin. Many of these neighborhoods lack electricity, running water, and a sewage system.

Living conditions in the colonias are very poor. For instance, the tiny Matamoros colonia called Privada Uniones is surrounded by chemical plants. Leaks from these plants have polluted the land and water around Privada Uniones, causing illnesses among its residents.

There are movements to change conditions in these colonias. Domingo González is a cofounder of the Texas-based Coalition for Justice in the Maquiladoras. He works to improve living conditions in the colonias. González has brought journalists and television crews to the colonias to report on the poor living conditions. He hopes his work will raise public awareness and force the chemical plants to clean up the pollution they have caused.

Active Learning: What questions would you ask residents of a colonia if you had the opportunity to interview them? Write down at least three questions.

3 An International Agreement

The United States and Mexico have been partners in trade for a long time. In 1993, their trade relationship changed. That was the year that Mexico, the United States, and Canada signed an historic agreement: the **North American Free Trade Agreement,** or **NAFTA.**

What is NAFTA?

NAFTA, which took effect on January 1, 1994, is a **free trade** agreement between the three countries. Free trade allows trade without tariffs, taxes, and other charges. Under NAFTA, Mexico, Canada, and the United States agreed to eliminate barriers to trade and investment. They agreed to allow goods to flow freely across their common borders for 15 years.

The Controversy over NAFTA

Getting NAFTA approved by the legislatures, or law-making bodies, of all three countries was no easy matter. NAFTA ultimately won passage, but there were many misgivings.

Mexican opponents claimed that the agreement favored the United States and Canada. In the United States, opposition to NAFTA came mainly from the industrial states in the north and east.

Opponents in the United States believed that NAFTA would encourage large corporations

---

Thinking It Over

1. How are the economies of sister cities along the U.S.-Mexican border linked?

2. **Understanding Causes and Effects** What has caused overcrowding along the border? What effects have overcrowding had on life along the U.S.-Mexican border?

to move their operations to Mexico, where labor costs were lower. They argued that many Americans were in danger of losing their jobs. Congressman David Bonior, a Democrat from the state of Michigan, voiced the concern of many when he told the House of Representatives, "It's not fair to ask American workers to compete against Mexican workers who earn $1 an hour."

On the other hand, supporters of NAFTA, such as Vice President Al Gore, argued that the treaty would actually create jobs in the United States because exports to Mexico and Canada would increase. This increase in exports would cause economic growth in all three countries.

Supporters of NAFTA also believed that the agreement might allow the United States and Mexico to work together to raise wages and improve environmental standards.

NAFTA's Present and Future

Now that NAFTA has been in effect for several years, it is clear that results are mixed. The treaty has not lived up to the high hopes of its supporters or the dark predictions of its opponents.

Initially, NAFTA caused an increase in trade. U.S. exports to Mexico increased by almost $16 billion. However, in 1995, there was a trade deficit because Mexico's economy had plunged.

NAFTA has had a positive effect on the maquiladoras, which have helped Mexico's economy. In the first two years after NAFTA took effect, employment in the maquiladora industry rose 20 percent to 648,000 workers. It is expected to reach 943,000 by the year 2000.

NAFTA seems to have had the greatest impact on the economies and people in northern Mexico. Its benefits are spreading to other parts of Mexico as well. According to José Luis Salas, a prominent Mexican businessman, "Americans invest in northern Mexico and northern Mexicans invest in southern Mexico." He adds: "It's not a bad deal."

However, some Mexican businesspeople would not agree with Salas. NAFTA has allowed large U.S. chains to build stores in Mexico. As a result, small businesses have suffered. The competition from these large chains often drives them out of business.

Some industries in the United States have suffered job losses as a result of NAFTA. When U.S. companies relocate to Mexico, many U.S.

In the early 1990s, there was much debate about NAFTA. Here, a group of Mexican Americans in Texas showed their opposition to NAFTA by staging a protest.

Both U.S. and Mexican citizens are concerned about water pollution. Industrial chemicals and raw sewage have made this river's waters unhealthy.

workers are laid off. This has fueled bad feelings among American workers about NAFTA and Mexicans. Among those who have suffered job losses are Mexican Americans.

Dealing with the Environment

NAFTA is supposed to deal with the environmental problems caused by a number of the maquiladoras. For example, the agreements between the United States and Mexico include rules about the proper disposal of hazardous waste. Such requirements are aimed at protecting the environment and improving conditions for workers.

However, some U.S. firms have chosen to ignore environmental laws. In such cases, communities on both sides of the border suffer the consequences. The border cities of Ciudad Juárez and El Paso are an example. They share the worst air pollution along the border. The pollution caused by U.S. firms on the Mexican side of the border affects both cities.

Mexamerica

NAFTA does more than ease trade among the nations of North America. The treaty helps to increase interaction between Mexico and the United States. This increased contact has led to the development of a vibrant new culture along the Río Grande. It is a culture that blends American and Mexican traditions. As a result, some call the borderlands "Mexamerica."

On both sides of the border, people hope that contact will have positive results, such as more jobs and a better standard of living. However, citizens of both countries are cautious. They know that throughout history, relations between their two nations have been somewhat strained. All must wait and see what the final results will be.

Thinking It Over

1. What are some of the arguments for and against NAFTA?
2. **Synthesizing Information** What role does free trade play in improving relations between the United States and Mexico?

GOING TO THE SOURCE

Living in a Colonia

Since 1965, U.S.-owned maquiladoras have sprung up in Mexico along the U.S.-Mexican border. Through the years, thousands of unemployed Mexicans have flocked to the northern borderlands in hopes of getting a job. The sudden increase in population has created a severe housing shortage. Workers build homes from whatever materials they can find. They often live in polluted areas near the factories. Below is a picture of the Colonia Cecilia Ocelli de Salinas in Matamoros. Study the picture and caption. Then answer the questions below.

Pollution is one of the most serious problems caused by the maquiladoras. Alongside this irrigation ditch is the Colonia Celcilia. The ditch has been polluted by chemicals dumped by maquiladoras located along the border.

1. How would you describe the conditions shown in this photograph?
2. **Drawing conclusions** How do you think living so close to industrial plants affects the quality of people's lives?

Case Study Review

Identifying Main Ideas

1. Why might some Mexicans support the establishment of maquiladoras in their country? Why might some oppose it?
2. Why has a border economy emerged along the U.S.-Mexico border?
3. Explain one benefit and one drawback of NAFTA to either the U.S. or Mexican economy.

Working Together

Work with a group to research a pair of the sister cities mentioned in this case study. Research the cities' history, population growth, and production. Find out what types of industries and businesses exist in the cities, when they were established, and how they are linked to businesses and industries on the other side of the border. Present your group's findings in a short report. Use graphs and other visual aids.

Active Learning

Interviewing Review the notes you took while reading this case study. Choose a classmate to work with and together decide who will be the subject of your mock interview. Write down seven to ten questions and think of possible answers based on who you are "interviewing." Then, decide who will be the interviewer and who will be the subject. Perform your mock interview for your class.

Lessons for Today

Domingo González is a community leader who struggles to improve living conditions in the colonias. One of his strategies is to get television stations and newspapers to report on the living conditions in the colonias. Do you think this is an effective way of bringing about change? Can television and newspaper coverage help his cause? Write a brief essay explaining your point of view.

What Might You Have Done?

Imagine you are a representative from your state serving in Congress during the debates to approve NAFTA. Would you be in favor of NAFTA or against it? What arguments would you use to support your views? Write a letter to the President justifying your point of view.

CRITICAL THINKING

Formulating and Supporting an Opinion

Supporting Ideas and Opinions

You know that it is important to use facts and details to support the main ideas in your writing. The quality of your writing depends on such a skill. It is also important to use sound reasons and examples to support your opinions. The quality of your thinking also depends on these skills. Take time to think through an opinion and be prepared to give reasons and examples to support it.

Critical thinkers learn how to analyze information and formulate and support their opinions. Now that you have read about NAFTA, decide what your opinion of it is. Based on what you have read, do you think it has helped or hurt the U.S. economy? How do you think it has affected Mexico's economy?

Use the graphic organizer below to help you sort out your thoughts on NAFTA. Then use it to help you think of facts to support your opinion. You will need to use information from this case study and from resources in your library to help you gather facts. First, copy the graphic organizer onto a sheet of paper. Then write a sentence in the center circle that describes your position on NAFTA. In the circles that surround the center circle, write facts that support your opinion. If you find more than four facts, just add more circles.

When you have completed the graphic organizer, use the information in it to outline an essay on NAFTA. When you write your essay, use the statement in the center circle to begin your introductory paragraph. Use the supporting facts to write three to four additional paragraphs. Finally, sum up your ideas in a concluding paragraph.

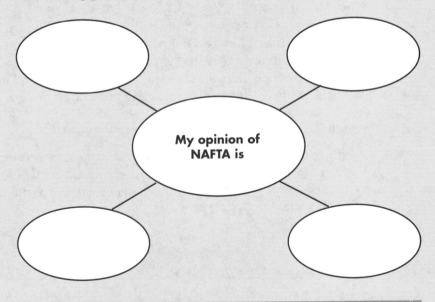

My opinion of NAFTA is

Proud of their Mexican heritage, Mexican Americans in Brooklyn, New York, celebrate Mexican Independence Day with a parade.

A FUTURE OF PROMISE AND HOPE

CRITICAL QUESTIONS

■ What are some common experiences of Mexican immigrants?

■ How has Mexican American culture influenced life in the United States?

TERMS TO KNOW

■ mural
■ demographers
■ undocumented immigrants
■ repatriate
■ bracero

ACTIVE LEARNING

A **mural** is a large wall painting that depicts a scene. Your assignment for the Follow-Up is to create a sketch of a mural that symbolizes the Mexican American experience. Read the hint boxes to help you plan your mural.

Our forebears [ancestors] dwelt in that blissful, happy place called Aztlán, which means "Whiteness." . . . There they lived in leisure, when they were called Mexitin and Azteca. There they had . . . great flocks of ducks of different kinds . . . They had . . . groves of trees along the edge of the waters. Our ancestors . . . made floating gardens upon which they sowed maize, chili, tomatoes, beans . . . and all kinds of seed which we now eat and which were brought from there.

This is how an Aztec described a place called Aztlán to a priest from Spain in the early 1580s. Aztlán was the original Aztec homeland. It was the place where the Aztecs had lived before they migrated south to central Mexico. In Mexico, they built a grand city called Tenochtitlán.

In the 1500s, conquerors from Spain destroyed Aztec civilization and built Mexico City on the ruins of Tenochtitlán. When the Spaniards heard about Aztlán, some explorers went in search of it. They never found the place. However, Aztlán remained a symbol of Mexico's Aztec heritage. Hundreds of years later, when Mexico won its independence from Spain in 1821, it used Aztlán as a symbol of liberty.

Today, no one knows exactly where Aztlán was located. Most believe it was somewhere in what is now the U.S. Southwest. Many Mexican Americans have strong feelings about Aztlán. In the 1960s and 1970s, Aztlán became a symbol of the Chicano Movement. (See Case Study 6.) For many, Aztlán represents a deep connection to their Mexican-Aztec heritage.

1 A Diverse Population

In the United States today, Mexican Americans are part of a larger group called Latinos. Latinos are people in the United States whose roots are in the Spanish-speaking countries of Latin America and the Caribbean. As you can see from the pie graph on page 119, Mexican Americans account for about 64 percent of all Latinos in the United States. **Demographers**, or scientists who study changes in the population, are predicting that in the 21st century, Latinos will be the largest group in the United States.

By 1994, there were over 17 million Mexican Americans. As one of the fastest growing ethnic groups, Mexican Americans will continue to gain influence in the United States and contribute to U.S. society. Although most Mexican Americans live in California and the Southwest, many have settled in other areas of the country, such as the Northeast and Northwest.

Like the members of any other ethnic group, the Mexican American community is quite diverse, or varied. Some Mexican American families have lived in the United States for hundreds of years. Others have just arrived. Some Mexican Americans come to this country well-educated and with professional careers. Others are poor farmers or factory workers. Some Mexican Americans speak only Spanish. Others speak only English. Despite these differences, most Mexican Americans share common values and experiences, such as a rich Mexican heritage, a commitment to family, and a hope of finding good jobs.

Seeking Economic Opportunity

The United States is a country of immigrants. Throughout U.S. history, people from all over the world have come to this country seeking a better life.

A number of Mexicans believe that by moving to the United States, they are simply returning to their ancient homeland of Aztlán. However, like immigrants of other cultures, most Mexicans come to the United States in search of work. Mexico's population has been rising at a rapid rate. Often there are not enough jobs for everyone. Many Mexicans hope to earn money and return home to take care of their families.

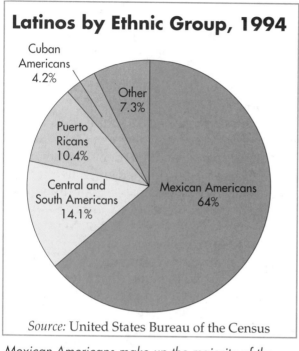

Latinos by Ethnic Group, 1994

Cuban Americans 4.2%

Other 7.3%

Puerto Ricans 10.4%

Central and South Americans 14.1%

Mexican Americans 64%

Source: United States Bureau of the Census

Mexican Americans make up the majority of the Latino population in the United States.

Rosa María Urbina, for example, left Mexico for El Paso, Texas, after her husband died. She could not afford to bring her three young children with her. As she explained:

> At the time, the economy in Mexico had become horrible. Inflation was going crazy. . . . My only hope was to cross the river to the United States. If I could find a job that paid enough money, my children could join me. I wanted them to have an education and a proper life . . . to be somebody.

Crossing the Border

In recent history, quotas have made legal immigration difficult. Those who are desperate take a chance and try to cross the border illegally, or without proper documentation. **Undocumented immigrants** have a difficult time finding work. They often must take the worst or most dangerous jobs for the lowest pay.

It is not easy to cross the U.S.-Mexico border without documents. The border is about 2,000 miles long. The seven main crossing points are very heavily guarded by the U.S. Border Patrol. In Mexico, the patrol is fearfully termed *La Migra,* short in Spanish for "migration."

Crossing the border was not always so difficult. In fact, at certain periods in U.S. history, Mexican immigration was welcomed and even encouraged. For example, during World War I (1914–1918), the United States experienced an economic boom and a labor shortage. Mexican immigration was encouraged until a serious economic depression hit the United States in the 1930s. This worldwide crisis was called the Great Depression. As work became scarce, many Anglos accused Mexican laborers of stealing jobs. Thousands of Mexicans were forced to **repatriate,** or return to their home country.

World War II (1939–1945) brought an end to the Depression. Once again, U.S. factories and farms needed workers. This time, the U.S. and Mexican governments set up the **bracero** program. The bracero program lasted from 1942 to 1964. Braceros were hired hands or laborers who came to work in the fields for certain periods of time. Then they returned to Mexico.

A Dual Identity

As you have read, the Mexican American community is diverse. Whether they are wealthy, poor, or in between, many Mexican Americans have two identities: their American identity and their Mexican identity.

Julio Guerrero, a Mexican American who has U.S. citizenship, works in Houston, but he lives in Monterrey, Mexico. He is a third-generation Mexican American who declares:

> I would fight and die in the American army if they called me. That's how much I love this country. But as a person, I feel Mexican, and I want my children to feel that way too, even though I hope they will come to live here when they are older. For now, they

come here to visit, but they'll stay in Mexico because it's easier, safer to raise them there.

Like many Americans who have emigrated to this country, Guerrero expresses strong feelings about both the United States and the country of his ancestors.

Active Learning: Think about how you can represent the great diversity of the Mexican American community in your mural.

Thinking It Over

1. What is the most common reason Mexicans emigrate to the United States?
2. **Applying Information** How have economic conditions in the United States affected Mexican immigration?

2 Gaining a Voice in the United States

Pride in their Mexican heritage and a commitment to improving their lives in the United States attracted many Mexican Americans to the Chicano Movement in the 1960s and 1970s. (See Case Study 6.) As a result of this movement, Mexican Americans gained increased political power and more freedom to exercise their civil rights. Today, Mexican Americans continue to fight against discrimination and prejudice. The Latino March of October 1996 is an example of this continued struggle.

Organizing to Gain Rights

On October 12, 1996, as many as 100,000 Latinos gathered in Washington, D.C., for the Latino March on Washington. The march aimed to publicize laws that affected immigration, education, and labor.

Latinos from all walks of life participated in this historic event. College student Hector García said that he and his friends came to the march "to show our elected officials that we have a vote and we're capable of putting them in office or taking them out of office."

Years before the Latino March on Washington, groups of Mexican Americans formed organizations to help fight against the discrimination and prejudice that affected them. You may recall the GI Forum in Case Study 4, the United Farm Workers in Case Study 5, and the Mothers of East Los Angeles in Case Study 7.

Today, Mexican Americans and other groups continue to work for a variety of issues that affect their lives. For example, in California during the past few years, students of all ages have led protests against state propositions, or plans, that would greatly limit their rights.

Power in Politics

As a result of the Chicano Movement, Mexican Americans have achieved a great deal in the political arena. Mexican Americans such as Katherine Ortega and Henry Cisneros have risen to high positions in the national government. Ortega became Treasurer of the United States in 1983. Cisneros was mayor of San Antonio and then served as Secretary of Housing and Urban Development during President Bill Clinton's first term. Both have worked to improve the lives of Mexican Americans.

Leaders in Business

Many people believe that economic opportunities also help strengthen a community. A number of Mexican Americans have excelled in business.

For example, Nancy E. Archuleta founded her own company, MEVATEC, in 1985. It is one of the fastest-growing Latino-owned businesses. MEVATEC supplies high-tech materials for the nation's Air Force and provides engineering services for the Defense Department.

Another outstanding Mexican American businessperson is Luis Nogales. During his youth, Nogales worked as a migrant farm worker. He became involved in the Chicano Movement during the 1960s and 1970s and later earned a law degree at Stanford University. He eventually became president of Univision, the Spanish-language TV network.

Leaders in Education

One of the legacies of the Chicano Movement was the establishment of Chicano Studies or Mexican American Studies departments in many universities. Leaders in the field of education such as Dr. Eugene Garcia, Dr. Lou Carranza, and Dr. José A. Carrasco have made tremendous contributions. The courses they developed have helped Mexican Americans to learn the value of their heritage and to use their knowledge to improve their lives in the future.

Thinking It Over

1. How have Mexican Americans continued to fight for equal rights in the 1990s?
2. **Making Inferences** How did the Chicano Movement help Mexican Americans get more involved in politics, business, and education?

Active Learning: In your murals, how might you bring to life the individuals you learned about in Section 2?

3 Mexican Culture in the United States

Rodeo. Fiesta. Chocolate. Tomato. Coyote. These are words that are used often in the United States and have their roots in the Spanish language. But language is not the only way in which Mexican culture has influenced U.S. culture. Other ways include architecture, art, music, the performing arts, and literature.

Art and Architecture

If you live in or have visited the states of Arizona, New Mexico, or Texas, you have no doubt seen examples of Mexican-style architecture. Houses with red-tiled roofs and white walls are common throughout the Southwest.

San Antonio, Texas, is a city that is 55 percent Mexican American. Its central library was designed by Mexican American architect Ricardo Legorreta. The building has red walls and covered terraces. It looks very much like buildings found in Mexico.

Another form of art for which Mexican Americans are well known is painting. A number of Mexican American painters have created murals, or large wall paintings, that depict a scene or scenes. The mural arose in Mexico after the Mexican Revolution in the early 20th century as a bright and expressive way to preserve history. This tradition is still alive today. Modern Mexican American muralists include Judy Baca, who helped pioneer the mural movement in Los Angeles.

Mexican American Literature

Mexican Americans have made outstanding contributions in literature. Sandra Cisneros and Gary Soto are well-known writers of fiction and poetry. Much of Soto's and Cisneros's writing describes what it is like to grow up as a Mexican American in the United States. Rudolfo Anaya is another well-known Mexican American writer. His novel *Bless Me, Ultima* gives readers an idea of the social customs and values of a Mexican American family in the Southwest.

The Performing Arts

Traditional Mexican music includes the mariachi band. Mariachi musicians stroll as they play guitars, brass instruments, and violins. Traditional Mexican music has influenced many current Mexican American musicians and bands, such as Carlos Santa, Los Lobos, and Selena.

Years ago, several Mexican American actors and actresses, including Rita Hayworth and Raquel Welch, changed their names. They feared that prejudice would bar them from success. Today, circumstances are different. Actors such as Edward James Olmos do not need to hide their heritage. Olmos, one of the most famous Mexican American actors, has starred in such films as *Alambrista, Stand and Deliver,* and *Selena.*

A Rich Past and a Bright Future

Clearly, a number of individual Mexican Americans have risen as stars in their fields. But it is as a group that Mexican Americans will continue to influence life in the United States. For Mexican Americans who took part in the Chicano Movement, the search for Aztlán was an important idea. They believed that Mexican Americans in the Southwest were struggling to rebuild their ancient homeland. Today, the search for Aztlán continues in a sense, as Mexican Americans start new lives and build strong communities in the Southwest and throughout the United States.

The mural is a traditional form of art that dates back to the Aztecs. This mural, created by Carlos Rosas is called "Evolution of a Young Chicano." It is painted on the side of the El Paso Boys and Girls Club building in south El Paso, Texas.

Case Study Review

Identifying Main Ideas

1. Describe the diversity of the Mexican American community.

2. What issues did the Latino March on Washington try to address?

3. Name an important Mexican American who contributed to politics, business, or the arts in the United States and describe his or her contribution.

Working Together

Work with two or three other students to create an illustrated biography for one of the people mentioned in the Follow-Up. Use library resources to find out more about the person you have chosen. Then create an outline and a first draft. Revise the draft and sketch one or two illustrations to accompany your biography.

Active Learning

Creating a Mural Work with two or three classmates to create a mural that reflects what you have read about in the Follow-Up. Review the notes you took while reading the Follow-Up. On a sheet of paper, sketch your initial ideas for the mural. List the materials you would need in order to complete the project. Review your sketch and revise it, if necessary. If possible, gather the materials you will need and create your mural.

Lessons for Today

An agenda is similar to a list of important things to do. Make a list of at least three issues you think a Mexican American politician's agenda should contain. Give reasons for each issue on your list.

What Might You Have Done?

Imagine that it is November of 1996. It has been one month since the Latino March on Washington. As a marcher and a Mexican American, you want to follow up with your local politicians on an important issue in the Latino community, such as education, immigration, or labor. First, identify the issue you wish to focus on and write a paragraph stating your opinion. Next, come up with a strategy for communicating your views on this issue to your representatives in the government.

GLOSSARY

Anglo a term that originally referred to Americans whose ancestors came from England; today it often refers to Americans whose background is from anywhere in Europe except Spain

annexed added

barrio a section of a city where there are large numbers of Latinos

bilingual to read and speak two different languages

boycott a refusal to buy a product until certain demands are met

bracero a contract laborer

Californios Mexicans who lived in California before it became part of the United States

Chicano a term that means Mexican American; developed in the 1960s, it was used to express Mexican American pride

coalition an alliance of many groups that are fighting a single issue

colonias poor neighborhoods in Mexico in which residents usually live in shacks without electricity or other conveniences

compromises settlements of a dispute in which each side gives in a little

Conservatives during the Mexican Revolution, people who wished to preserve the existing power structure and the influence of the Church

Criollos in the days of Spanish control, people born in the Americas to Spanish parents

cryptographers code-breakers

defect to switch sides

demographer a scientist who studies changes in the population

deport to send away

ejido a group of villagers who farmed their land together

El Movimiento the Chicano movement

epidemic a rapidly spreading disease

evict to force out

free trade trade that is free of tariffs, taxes, and other charges

GI Bill a law instituted after World War II that guaranteed veterans a number of benefits including low-cost housing and four years of education

grassroots on the local level; usually referring to grassroots organizations, or organizations run by local people

guerrilla a soldier who fights in a small group that surprises its enemies by staging hit-and-run raids

haciendas large ranches or estates

immunization the process of giving medicine to make a person's body able to resist certain illnesses

inauguration the formal beginning of an elected official's term of office

incinerator a large furnace that burns trash

indigenous people who are native to a land

Indios the term commonly used in Mexico to refer to indigenous, or native, peoples of Mexico

labor union an organization that fights for better conditions for workers

La Raza the race; the Mexican American people

Latinos U.S. citizens whose roots lie in Spanish-speaking lands south of the United States

legacy something valuable that is handed down from an older generation to a younger generation

Liberals during the Mexican Revolution, people who supported reforms, including reducing the power of the Church

lobby to seek to influence public officials to pass new laws

manifest destiny the U.S. policy that aimed to expand the nation's borders from the Atlantic ocean to the Pacific ocean

maquiladora a factory in Mexico that is foreign-owned

Mestizos people whose parents were of mixed Spanish and Indio background

migrant worker a worker who moves from place to place to find seasonal employment

migration movement from one place to another

moratorium the stopping of all work and activity in protest

mural a large wall painting that depicts a scene or scenes

NAFTA (North American Free Trade Agreement) a free trade agreement that took effect on January 1, 1994, between the United States, Mexico, and Canada

Patriots American colonists who fought for independence from Britain

placer mining a method of finding gold by washing soil and gravel from a river

ranchos huge estates on which large herds of cattle were raised

reforms improvements or changes

repatriate to return a person to his or her home country

satire using humor, or biting wit, to mock someone

squatters people who occupy land illegally and may try to claim it for their own

strike a walkout by workers from their place of employment, usually to protest working conditions

tariffs taxes on imported goods

toxic poisonous

undocumented immigrant someone who enters a country without proper documentation

vaccinations medicines that can prevent serious diseases

vaqueros Mestizo or Indio cattle herders or cowboys

Zapatistas followers of Emiliano Zapata

INDEX

ACKNOWLEDGMENTS

Grateful acknowledgment is made to the following publishers, authors, and other copyright holders:

p. 78: *Field* and *Field Poem* by Gary Soto in *Mexican American Literature,* pp. 525-528. Copyright © 1990, Harcourt Brace Jovanovich, Publishers. We eagerly invite the publisher to contact Globe Fearon Educational Publisher to arrange for the customary publishing transactions.

p. 90: "Are You a Chicano?" in *The Mexican American Family Album* by Dorothy and Thomas Hoobler. Copyright © 1994, Oxford University Press. We eagerly invite the publisher to contact Globe Fearon Educational Publisher to arrange for the customary publishing transactions.

p. 102: "Vernon Victory" by Juana Beatriz Gutierrez in the *Los Angeles Times*, June 24, 1991, p. B-4. Used by permission of Juana Beatriz Gutierrez.

Grateful acknowledgment is made to the following for illustrations, photographs, and reproductions on the pages indicated:

Photo Credits: **Cover:** George Rodriguez, George Ballis/ Take Stock; **Title Page:** George Ballis/ Take Stock; **p. 5:** George Rodriguez; **p. 7:** Corbis-Bettmann; **p. 10:** Jeff Greenberg, Archive Photos; **p. 13:** Archive Photos; **p. 15:** Laurie Platt Winfrey, Carousel; **p. 20:** Archive Photos; **p. 22:** Bancroft Library; **p. 24:** Superstock Henry E. Huntington Library, DAG #55; **p. 27:** Corbis-Bettmann; **p. 33:** Corbis-Bettmann; **p. 34:** Laurie Platt Winfrey; **p. 35:** Laurie Platt Winfrey; **p. 36:** The Granger Collection; **p. 40:** The Granger Collection; **p. 41:** The Granger Collection; **p. 44:** UPI/Corbis-Bettmann; **p. 46:** UPI/Bettmann; **p. 48:** Culver Pictures; **p. 50:** Corbis-Bettmann; **p. 54:** UPI/Corbis-Bettmann; **p. 56:** UPI/Corbis-Bettmann; **p. 58:** U.S. Army Photograph; **p. 60:** Arizona Historical Society/Tucson 63,527; **p. 62:** George Rodriguez; **p. 63:** George Rodriguez; **p. 67:** Courtesy of the Archives of Labor and Urban Affairs, Wayne State University; **p. 71:** Courtesy of the Archives of Labor and Urban Affairs, Wayne State University; **p. 72:** Courtesy of the Archives of Labor and Urban Affairs, Wayne State University; **p. 73:** George Ballis/Take Stock; **p. 76:** Corbis-Bettmann; **p. 77:** Wide World Photos; **p. 81:** UPI/Corbis-Bettmann; **p. 83:** Matt Heron/Take Stock; **p. 84:** George Rodriguez; **p. 86:** George Rodriguez; **p. 93:** Herald Examiner Collection, Los Angeles Public Library; **p. 94:** Los Angeles Times; **p. 96:** George Rodriguez; **p. 98:** Herald Examiner Collection, Los Angeles Public Library; **p. 101:** Judy Branfman; **p. 105:** David Maung, Impact Visuals; **p. 108:** Jack Kurtz, Impact Visuals; **p. 112:** Fred Chase, Impact Visuals; **p. 113:** John W. Emmons, Impact Visuals; **p. 114:** Jim Saah, Impact Visuals; **p. 117:** George Rodriguez; **p. 119:** Jack Kurtz, Impact Visuals; **p. 122:** Michael Kaufman, Impact Visuals.